S0-AJH-592

Martin Kramer
EDITOR-IN-CHIEF

Conflict Management in Higher Education

Susan A Holton
Bridgewater State College

EDITOR

Number 92, Winter 1995

JOSSEY-BASS PUBLISHERS
San Francisco

CONFLICT MANAGEMENT IN HIGHER EDUCATION
Susan A Holton (ed.)
New Directions for Higher Education, no. 92
Volume XXIII, Number 4
Martin Kramer, Editor-in-Chief

Microfilm copies of issues and articles are available in 16mm and 35mm, as well as microfiche in 105mm, through University Microfilms Inc., 300 North Zeeb Road, Ann Arbor, Michigan 48106-1346.

ISSN 0271-0560   ISBN 0-7879-9942-3

NEW DIRECTIONS FOR HIGHER EDUCATION is part of The Jossey-Bass Higher and Adult Education Series and is published quarterly by Jossey-Bass Inc., Publishers, 350 Sansome Street, San Francisco, California 94104-1342. Second-class postage paid at San Francisco, California, and at additional mailing offices. POSTMASTER: Send address changes to New Directions for Higher Education, Jossey-Bass Inc., Publishers, 350 Sansome Street, San Francisco, California 94104-1342.

SUBSCRIPTIONS for 1995 cost $48.00 for individuals and $64.00 for institutions, agencies, and libraries.

EDITORIAL CORRESPONDENCE should be sent to the Editor-in-Chief, Martin Kramer, 2807 Shasta Road, Berkeley, California 94708-2011.

Cover photograph and random dot by Richard Blair/Color & Light © 1990.

TCF Manufactured in the United States of America on Lyons Falls Pathfinder Tradebook. This paper is acid-free and 100 percent totally chlorine-free.

CONTENTS

EDITOR'S NOTES

It became so predictable that I was surprised if anyone responded differently. When I revealed the topic of my research, academics almost always responded "Conflict? In higher education? Surely not!" While most were being sarcastic, their responses, and the uniformity of the responses, showed that this is an issue that has long been hidden—and that can no longer be ignored.

As academics, we are supposedly above it all somehow. People suggest that academics, who are undeniably intelligent people, should be able to handle disputes and disagreements. We should not have conflicts. But we do. Anytime two or more people—especially people of different values, disciplines, and interests—gather, there will be conflict. And academics are no different.

There is conflict in all facets of life, including the professional lives of academics. It is necessary, first, to acknowledge that conflict exists, and that it is inevitable, especially in a setting where independent thought is encouraged. There is a sense, often articulated, that because of the nature of the academy, conflict should be cloaked. However, it must be acknowledged. "The spirit of collegiality does not free these institutions from difficult conflicts that can jeopardize the educational process, undermine creative scholarship or threaten individual careers" (Folger and Shubert, 1986, p. 5).

Conflict can be either destructive or constructive. The likelihood that it will be constructive is increased when it is openly acknowledged, analyzed, and dealt with. In their work on conflict, Blake, Mouton, and Williams (1981, p. 5) acknowledged the importance of dealing with conflict at the university: "Conflict is inevitable in a setting where people have different points of view and freedom of expression is encouraged. The effects of conflict can be either disruptive and destructive or creative and constructive, depending upon whether the persons involved can work toward mutual understanding or simply an agreement to differ without disrespect. Inability to cope with conflict constructively and creatively leads to increased hostility, antagonism, and divisiveness. Clear thinking disintegrates, and prejudice and dogmatism come to prevail. This is the antithesis of the university norm of 'reasoned discourse.' "

In these days of often chaotic change within institutions of higher education, conflict is inevitable. It is thus vital that we understand the dynamics of conflict and effective ways to deal with it.

The term *conflict management*, rather than *conflict resolution,* is used throughout this volume. I believe that conflict is rarely truly "resolved." We need only think about the times when we were young, when siblings or friends did something to hurt us. The fact that we can recall such childhood events suggests that those conflicts may have been managed but they were not totally resolved.

The purpose of this volume is to look at conflict within the academy, to analyze it, to understand it, and to discover ways to manage it. In Chapter One, I provide an overview of conflict and conflict management. In Chapter Two, I examine the fascinating history of conflict in higher education, tracing the phenomenon from the earliest roots of Hellenic education through the establishment of higher education in the United States. From this historical perspective, I then consider the issues that are faced by today's faculty.

Faculty-to-faculty conflict is the focus of Chapter Three, by Ray Leal. He looks at conflict as a result of the faculty enterprise, of current tensions in academia, and of the organizational culture in which we all work.

Conflict among students has long been a concern for the academy. In Chapter Four, Jacqueline Gibson examines typical student conflicts and describes ways to manage them.

Department chairs have one of the most difficult jobs on campus. In Chapter Five, Walter Gmelch looks at the institutional, interpersonal, and positional conflicts faced by chairs.

The search for an author for a chapter on faculty-administrator conflict seemed endless. I was told, more than once, "I wouldn't touch that!" I was also told by a few administrators that they were not in a place in their careers where it was "safe" to write such a chapter. Those responses alone demonstrate the importance of faculty and administrators finding positive ways to manage conflict. Gerald Phillips, an emeritus professor and a wise man who had filled numerous faculty and administrator roles, agreed to write the chapter. I was overjoyed because he was known within the discipline of communication to be an honest critic of the world. We worked together on the chapter's contents, and he was in the process of writing it when he died. To complete Chapter Six, I took Phillips's ideas and elaborated on them.

One of the most public conflicts in higher education is that among collective bargaining units. Frank R. Annunziato, in Chapter Seven, explores the current state of academic collective bargaining.

In Chapter Eight, Alan W. Ostar takes a "mega-view" of institutional conflict. He examines the complex roots of conflict as they relate to the competing claims and issues of parties that compose the institution as a whole.

The world of academia does not stop at the doors of our institution. Since the beginning of the academy, we have had town-and-gown conflict. In Chapter Nine, Wallace Warfield focuses on conflict between the college or university and its host community.

What are the current trends of conflict management in higher education? William C. Warters, in Chapter Ten, addresses the latest programs in higher education.

Given all of this conflict, how do we deal with it? Some answers are provided in Chapter Eleven as I reflect on the Holton Model of Conflict Management and explain three main parts of conflict management: identification of the conflict, identification of solutions, and implementation of solutions.

What is the future of conflict in higher education? What do academic institutions need to do to create a positive, constructive atmosphere where conflict is a positive, motivating force? In the final chapter, I address these questions.

In the volume's Appendix, over a hundred conflict management programs at institutions of higher education in the United States and Canada are listed. This is a beginning list. Institutions are encouraged to contact me to add their names to the data base, which will be updated every semester. An information packet about each of the programs is also available through the Project on Conflict in Higher Education at Bridgewater State College.

Finally, I want to acknowledge the efforts of my two research assistants. I thank graduate student Donna Polleys and undergraduate student Jessica Kelly for their hours of labor in significantly assisting in the work of this volume.

Susan A Holton
Editor

References

Blake, R. R., Mouton, J. S., and Williams, M. S. *The Academic Administrator Grid: A Guide to Developing Effective Management Teams.* San Francisco: Jossey-Bass, 1981.

Folger, J. P., and Shubert, J. J. *Resolving Student-Initiated Grievances in Higher Education: Dispute Resolution Procedures in a Non-Adversarial Setting.* National Institute for Dispute Resolution Report No. 3. Washington, D.C.: National Institute for Dispute Resolution, 1986.

SUSAN A HOLTON is professor of communication studies at Bridgewater State College, Bridgewater, Massachusetts, and director of the Massachusetts Faculty Development Consortium.

Conflict is inherent to every social system, including higher education. A clear definition of conflict, and an understanding of why conflict exists, will help us to manage conflict.

Conflict 101

Susan A Holton

Before conflict can be managed, it must be understood. Donohue and Kolt (1992, p. 4) defined conflict as "a situation in which interdependent people express (manifest or latent) differences in satisfying their individual needs and interests, and they experience interference from each other in accomplishing these goals." This definition includes elements of conflict that can be found in any organizational context, including higher education. There must be interdependence. Faculty, administrators, staff, and students need one another; interdependence is a given in higher education.

Conflict can be manifest or latent; it can be openly expressed or hidden from view. Much of the conflict in higher education has been hidden. Joan Stark, faculty member, former dean, and educational researcher, has noted that "conflict in the academy is not overt. . . . Faculty will fight within the departments, not outside. If the dean sees faculty unable to get along and govern themselves, the dean will reward the department less well because they can't 'get their own stuff together.' If the chips are down, faculty members will defend each other but in private, will fight with each other. When those fights become public, they become dysfunctional" (personal communication, March 20, 1995).

The differences between public and private conflicts are significant. The private nature of much of the conflict in higher education makes it dynamically different from conflict in other, more public organizational contexts. In their book *Hidden Conflict in Organizations: Uncovering Behind-the-Scenes Disputes* Kolb and Bartunek (1992) focus on latent conflict. In distinguishing public and private conflicts, they observed,

> In public conflicts, the norms and procedures for reaching an equitable settlement surface through formally derived laws, written documents, and public

norms. . . . Private disputes occur as covert or hidden conflict, often fused with other activities. Consequently, they are rarely labeled or authorized as disputes. Indeed they may be read as sabotage and disloyalty. The preferred modes of conflict management in the private sphere include avoidance, accommodation, tolerance, or "behind the scenes" coalition building. Disputants choose to ignore one another or forget about the grievance. They may think that they cannot change the system; hence they rely on private grievances as the primary mode of conflict management. In the private arena, norms and rules for appropriate conflict behavior arise from the situation rather than from public standards or bureaucratic rules [Kolb and Bartunek, 1992, p. 19].

It has been suggested by many that conflict in higher education has been latent for years. It is because of the present crises in academia that for many conflicts the latent has become manifest.

The needs and interests mentioned in Donohue and Kolt's (1992) definition of conflict can be either concrete, such as the need for an adequate office space, or more abstract, such as the need for respect and dignity. Conflict may also result from differences in the goals for a department, school, or college, or even for a classroom. It may also involve a need for power, and a resistance to someone who is perceived to have more power.

Finally, conflict is based on interference—or perceived interference. As long as the parties involved in conflict see one another as standing in the way of achieving a goal—regardless of whether each is in fact blocking another's goal achievement—then there is interference.

The definition of conflict also includes discontinuity of interests. "Every form of social conflict implies that one or both parties perceive their interests as divergent—whether or not they are, in reality, divergent . . . any conflict signifies some degree of perceived incompatibility between the parties' goals, or between their preferred means of achieving similar goals" (Levinger and Rubin, 1994, p. 202).

In order to manage conflict in higher education, it is recommended that the conflicted groups work toward a common definition of their goals. Often, conversation will reveal that the goals are not as divergent as the parties assumed, that there is not a significant discontinuity of interests. But until the parties sit down to listen to one another, that common ground will not be recognized.

Approaches to Conflict Management

Over the years, approaches to conflict within organizations have changed drastically. In the earliest days of organizational theory, the traditional approach to organizational conflict saw conflict as destructive, something that must be eliminated within the organization. "In higher education, this remains the predominant view. . . . While there are exceptions to this generalization, they only serve to accentuate the predominant negative belief that conflict emanates from ill disposition rather than constructive dialogue" (Gmelch and Carroll, 1991, p. 109).

In the 1950s, the organizational perspective on conflict was altered to the behavioral approach, which saw conflict as natural and which encouraged people to accept conflict as an inevitable part of working together. "Behavioral philosophies still assume the need to reduce conflict, although the strategies to accomplish this end require changing people's attitudes and behaviors" (Gmelch and Carroll, 1991, p. 110).

Today, organizations take a "principled approach," based on the work of Fisher and Ury (1981). This approach says that conflict is a necessary part of organizations and that dealing with conflict should be encouraged. Some within higher education are beginning to acknowledge the importance of this principled approach. Yet, in their perception of conflict, and of the ways of managing it, many people are stuck in a pre-1950s traditional approach, hoping that conflict will go away.

Why Does Conflict Exist?

Most conflict management research focuses on three different sources of conflict: conflict over resources, conflict over needs, and conflict over values. Conflict over resources, a type that has increased in frequency in higher education over the last few years, occurs when two or more people want something that is scarce. There may be one computer, and five faculty who want it; or a dozen parking spaces, and fifty people who work in the adjacent building. Conflict over needs is more intangible and therefore more difficult to resolve. This type of conflict includes the needs for power, for belonging, for achievement, and for self-esteem. Unfortunately, within the academy and within the world at large, these needs often seem to be "zero-sum" needs: If one person has power, then another cannot have it. In reality, however, satisfaction of these needs is not zero sum but rather in unending supply. All of us can have power, all of us can achieve self-esteem. But achievement of each of these needs is not easy. The third type, conflict over values, is the most difficult of all and often seems to be the most threatening within a department, a division, or an institution. This type includes conflicts over the mission of the institution, over the goals of the department, and over what is politically appropriate for the division.

Another way to identify the types of conflict is to look at the underlying motives in conflict. Levinger and Rubin (1994) have suggested that all conflicts have one or more of three underlying motives: competition, cooperation, and individualism. At the extreme, the competition motive suggests that one wishes to win at the expense of another. In competition, both parties cannot win; it is the classic case of win-lose. Cooperation, on the other hand, suggests that both parties work together, with the goal of win-win. And individualism focuses solely on the work of one person, who does not care whether another wins or loses. "Most conflicts are not purely any of those, but are a mix of more than one, especially in a relationship where there is some interdependence" (Levinger and Rubin, 1994, p. 204).

The culture of higher education makes the competition-individualism mode of conflict much too prevalent. Faculty often work alone and thus fall into the individualism mode. Individuals, departments, and divisions are often told that the reward structure is a zero-sum game; if department X gets a new system, department Y will not be able to. Thus, much of higher education does not operate in the cooperative, win-win mode. As I note in Chapter Twelve of this volume, an atmosphere of community and a common commitment to the institution, now sought by many in higher education, will facilitate establishment and maintenance of the cooperative mode. Moreover, as institutions actively engage in strategic planning, a process that should make obvious the interdependence of all parts of the institution, the importance of cooperation will become more obvious.

Conflict is social interaction. Some theorists identify conflict as a distinct cultural event within an organization, one that includes norms about how and when to fight and the topics for the fight. As such, conflict within the culture of the academy is different from conflict within any other type of organization. "Disputes are cultural events, evolving within a framework of rules about what is worth fighting for, what is the normal or moral way to fight, what kinds of wrongs warrant action, and what kinds of remedies are acceptable. . . . Ideas about how to respond to grievances are linked with socially constructed definitions of normal behavior, respectability, responsibility and the good person" (Merry and Silbey, 1984, p. 158). What is important to fight over in the academy may not be issues in other types of organizations.

Louis Pondy (1992), after years of serving as chair of an academic department, proposed a model of organizational conflict. He saw all organizations as systems of pure conflict in which conflicts are perpetuated without ever being resolved. "Organizations consist of numerous pairs of opposite tendencies (e.g., risk-taking and risk-avoiding, creativity and efficiency). If there were no active conflicts within these pairs, then one of the polar extremes would gradually become dominant in each case, the diversity of behavioral repertoire available to the organization would diminish, the organization would lose its capacity for adaptation in the face of environmental change, and it would run a high risk of eventual failure" (Pondy, 1992, p. 260). Thus, conflict is not only functional for an organization but also essential to its very existence. It is inevitable and even healthy for an organization.

What Are the Results of Conflict?

"Peace at any price" should not be the guiding principle of conflict management. Too often, conflict is seen only as a negative when, in fact, it can be energizing and productive. Some researchers have even suggested that too little conflict within an organization can stifle growth and productivity.

It is necessary to see the potential for positive change from conflict in higher education. As McCarthy (1980, p. 1) observed,

> Many educators are reluctant to acknowledge the presence of specific conflicts involving them on their own campuses. . . . This defensive reaction to conflict fails to take into account the fundamental and necessary role conflict plays in preserving existing institutional arrangements and, when managed productively, in encouraging individual and institutional adjustments to newly emerging forces and changing circumstances. What is worse, the failure to acknowledge the existence of conflict and the related hope that time or events will resolve disputes often exacerbates hostility and leads to destructive confrontation that could be avoided if the conflict were recognized, the issues examined, and the differences managed in a way that encourages cooperative problem-solving.

Along with cooperative problem solving, dealing with conflict within the academy can serve additional functions. Johnson, Johnson, and Smith (1989) noted five positive functions: (1) a unifying function resulting from increased group cohesiveness, (2) a group-preserving function resulting from prevention of accumulated hostility, (3) an integrative function resulting from stabilization following conflict, (4) a growth function resulting from the promotion of innovation, creativity, and change, and (5) a problem-solving function resulting from facilitation of the process of problem solving. In sum, departments, schools, and institutions that engage in conflict management have the opportunity to go from the chaos of conflict to the resultant group-enhancing management.

Conflict is inevitable in academia and in all other organizations, and it will only increase as we become more diverse in the populations of all sectors of the academic world. "Elimination of conflict would mean the elimination of such differences. The goal of conflict management is, for us, better conceived as the acceptance and enhancement of differences among persons and groups" (Bennis, Benne, and Chen, 1969, p. 152).

References

Bennis, W. G., Benne, K. D., and Chen, R. *The Planning of Change*. Troy, Mo.: Holt, Rinehart & Winston, 1969.

Donohue, W. A., and Kolt, R. *Managing Interpersonal Conflict*. Thousand Oaks, Calif.: Sage, 1992.

Fisher, R., and Ury, W. *Getting to Yes: Negotiating Agreement Without Giving In*. Boston: Houghton Mifflin, 1981.

Gmelch, W. H., and Carroll, J. B. "The Three Rs of Conflict Management for Department Chairs and Faculty." *Innovative Higher Education*, 1991, 16 (2), 107–123.

Johnson, D. W., Johnson, R. T., and Smith, K. "Controversy Within Decision-Making Situations." In M. A. Rahim (ed.), *Managing Conflict: An Interdisciplinary Approach*. New York: Praeger, 1989.

Kolb, D., and Bartunek, J. M. (eds.). *Hidden Conflict in Organizations: Uncovering Behind-the-Scenes Disputes.* Thousand Oaks, Calif.: Sage, 1992.

Levinger, G., and Rubin, J. Z. "Bridges and Barriers to a More General Theory of Conflict." *Negotiation Journal,* 1994, *10,* 201–215.

McCarthy, J. (ed.). *Conflict and Mediation in the Academy.* New Directions for Higher Education, no. 32. San Francisco: Jossey-Bass, 1980.

Merry, S. E., and Silbey, S. S. "What Do Plaintiffs Want? Reexamining the Concept of Dispute." *Justice System Journal,* 1984, *9* (2), 151–178.

Pondy, L. R. "Reflections on Organizational Conflict." *Journal of Organizational Behavior,* 1992, *13,* 257–261.

SUSAN A HOLTON is professor of communication studies at Bridgewater State College, Bridgewater, Massachusetts, and director of the Massachusetts Faculty Development Consortium.

Conflict has been a part of higher education since its inception. Many problems faced today by academics have centuries-old prototypes.

It's Nothing New! A History of Conflict in Higher Education

Susan A Holton

Pythagoras established the first Hellenic institution of higher education. During these earliest times of Hellenic higher education, conflict caused the demise of the school when enemies "suppressed it and dispersed its adherents" (Cowley and Williams, 1991, p. 4).

The school of Isocrates began in 392 B.C. but did not survive. In the first recorded instance of administrator-faculty conflict, Isocrates, in his inaugural address, "inveighed against those teachers who betrayed their high calling by coaching their students in verbal trickery and by inculcating low morals in general" (Cowley and Williams, 1991, p. 7).

Aristotle, like many others, thought that he would become the head of the academy when Plato died. But this did not happen. He left the academy and Athens, only to return in 338 to establish the Lyceum. Conflict later caused Aristotle to flee Athens again when suspicious citizens forced the closing of his school.

Higher education has always had to deal with the intrusion of the outside world. In the early days of Alexandria, Hadrian's mother, Plotina, meddled in the affairs of the Epicurean school in Athens. In Rome, the emperors retained the right to select the occupants of the learned chairs that they endowed (Cramer, 1939).

Often, rules dictated the content of the academies. In the Byzantine Empire, Leo III destroyed schools where the teaching disagreed with his ideas. Justinian, in A.D. 529, "forbade the teaching of philosophy and law in Athens so that the intellectual resources of the time would be concentrated in Constantinople" (Cowley and Williams, 1991, p. 28).

The University of Bologna was established because of conflict among faculty, students, merchants, and politicians. The faculty of Bologna organized into faculty guilds and "some of the professors joined forces with the city government against the students, the common enemy of both. . . . [They] got the town to appoint them public professors" (Cowley and Williams, 1991, p. 45). They received salaries from the public purse, thus establishing the first lay boards of supervision.

Faculties' need for some control in medieval universities was understandable. "[The professor] has to swear obedience to the students. If he wished a leave of absence for a single day, he had first to humbly request it of our students, then have the permission approved by the rector and the student council. If he failed to get five students for an 'ordinary' lecture or three for an 'extraordinary' one, he was declared absent and fined. If his popularity waned, he might bribe students to attend his lectures. . . . He was fined if he skipped a chapter or a decretal or if he postponed a troublesome question to the end of his lecture in the hope of submerging it in the bell's clamor. . . . A committee of students kept close watch on him 'for his spiritual good' " (Bishop, n.d., p. 69).

Conflict has always been a fact of life in academic institutions throughout the world. Immanuel Kant addressed the theme of faculty conflict in 1794. In *The Conflict of the Faculties* he discussed the turf war "between the 'lower' or philosophical faculty on the one hand and the three 'higher' faculties of theology, law and medicine on the other" (Kant, [1794] 1979, p. vii).

Conflict was a part of many of the early institutions of higher education in the United States. The first U.S. university was Harvard, first only because of a town-and-gown conflict. "George Thorpe attempted to establish Henrico College in 1619 but the Indians soon put an end to his ambitious enterprise by scalping him and sixteen of his tenants" (Slosson, [1921] 1991, p. 81). The institution was founded as William and Mary in 1693, fifty-seven years after Harvard.

Yale was founded in 1701, also because of conflict. The governing board of ten ministers (nine of them graduates of Harvard) wanted to be sure that this new college would avoid the liberal religion espoused at Harvard.

The University of Pennsylvania was established through a series of conflicts. In 1740, Benjamin Franklin and other citizens took over George Whitefield's Charity School, renamed it the College and Academy of Philadelphia in 1755, and, in 1791, it became the University of Pennsylvania. However, the conflicts within that institution were not over. In 1779, the legislature took over the powers of the school on the grounds that former trustees had proved hostile to the new government and that all denominations had not received equal treatment (Cowley and Williams, 1991, p. 81).

At Dartmouth College a split was evident when the president published a pamphlet attacking the board "for its conduct of College affairs." The board then published its own pamphlet in response and, in 1815, dismissed John Wheelock from the presidency. Subsequent appeals of the case to the U.S.

Supreme Court decided that higher education should be kept in the hands of private enterprise (Cowley and Williams, 1991, p. 119).

The conflict between research and teaching was articulated in a dispute among scientists, classicists, and religionists at Oxford and Cambridge. People "looked with unconcealed disdain upon what they considered to be the spiritually unprofitable and potentially heretical grubbings of the scientists" (Cowley and Williams, 1991, p. 140).

Conflict early in the twentieth century led to the establishment of faculty unions. In 1913, the American Association of University Professors (AAUP) was born when Professor Arthur Loveloy and associates at Johns Hopkins wrote to colleagues proposing the formation of a national professorial organization that would be designed "to promote a more general and methodological discussion of educational problems of the university; to create means for the authoritative expression of public opinion of the profession; and to make possible collective action, on occasions when such action seems called for" (American Association of University Professors, [1914] 1991, p. 458).

Student Conflict

Students have always rebelled and challenged the patience and wits of faculty and administrators. In medieval times they were forbidden to "shout, hiss, make noise, throw stones in class or deputize one's servant to do so." In the 1300s, the bishop in the Episcopal Court of Paris said, "They attend classes but make no effort to learn anything. . . . They frequently learn what had better be unknown. . . . They defraud their masters. . . . They have among themselves evil and disgraceful societies. . . . They contract debts and sometimes withdraw from the university without paying them" (Bishop, n.d., p. 72).

At Harvard, student uprisings were frequent. "The Great Rebellion of 1823 involved battles in commons, bonfires and explosions in the Yard, cannon balls from upper windows, drowning out of Tutor's voices in the classrooms, drenching people with buckets of ink and water and more" (Cowley and Williams, 1991, p. 105).

Yale was ripe with town-and-gown riots. In 1841, the students of Yale staged the first "Firemen's Riots," a street fight in which students reportedly cut a fire hose into small pieces, overturned the engine, and strewed fire-fighting apparatus about the town and yard. Eleven years later, a group of "townies" objected to the conduct of a number of undergraduates at a New Haven theatre. A fight followed in which a local bartender, whom a student struck with a dagger, was killed (Cowley and Williams, 1991). Students also expressed their displeasure with the faculty. "The students were wont to express their displeasure with their tutors by stoning their windows and attacking them with clubs if they chanced out after dark" (Fulton and Thompson, 1991, p. 9).

Since the earliest times, administrators have been trying to understand the reasons for campus unrest. "During the nineteenth century, discontent usually focused on such issues as poor food, inadequate housing, and excessively strict parietal rules; thus it was generally apolitical and parochial" (Astin, Astin, Bayer, and Bisconti, 1975, p. 17). Other authors noted that they rioted because of the reportedly poor recitation methods of the professors, the state curriculum, the rotting food and the "constant snooping of faculty members into their personal lives" (Cowley and Williams, 1991).

The riots of the students did cause changes in their institutions. In fact, athletics owes its origins to student riots. "Student riots and rebellions along with declining enrollments caused college authorities to approve of athletics and other outlets for the excess energies of students" (Cowley and Williams, 1991, p. 107).

During the Cold War, a different kind of conflict occurred within the academy. The McCarthy era was a time when faculty were dismissed after investigations into their past work. "It was commonplace to hear about campus investigations of alleged political radicals and of firings, near firings or forced resignations" (Lewis, 1988, p. 2).

Campus Conflict of the 1960s and 1970s

For many today, talk of conflict in higher education focuses on the campus riots and student rebellion of the 1960s and 1970s. Researchers have looked for underlying reasons for these conflicts. Joseph Califano, Jr. (1970, p. 147) reported that student protest involved "small numbers of hard-core radical students, fuzzy objectives reflecting a crisis of belief, time for revolt provided by affluence, a search for alternatives to a complex, technologically based life."

Astin, Astin, Bayer, and Bisconti (1975, p. 180), in writing about campus conflicts, concluded, "The occurrence of unrest on a particular campus was clearly not a random event; rather there were identifiable antecedent conditions that influenced the likelihood that protests would develop. . . . This depended less on specific policies and practices of that institution than on the characteristics of its student body and faculty." This earlier campus unrest continues to impact the academy today, "from dramatic changes in student enrollments, student views, and student life to the revolutionary curriculum approaches" (Astin, Astin, Bayer, and Bisconti, 1975, p. 2).

Admission of the "Others"

Most institutions of higher education were founded with Caucasian males in mind. Significant conflict occurred when "others" were admitted. "Most scholars tend to make the late 1960s as the beginning of the changes in diversity in higher education. It is important to recognize, however, that colleges and universities have been adjusting to and accommodating 'new' kinds of students almost since their founding" (Smith, 1989, p. 3).

Women were first admitted to institutions of higher education in 1837 at Oberlin College in Ohio, more than two hundred years after the founding of

Harvard. Vassar, the first women's college, was established in 1865, followed by Smith and Wellesley in 1875 and Bryn Mawr and Mount Holyoke in the 1880s. By 1900, 70 percent of the colleges in the United States were coeducational, and women constituted 30 percent of the student body in higher education (Chamberlain, 1988, p. 4). In 1991, 50 percent of the undergraduates were women, 25 percent of the faculty were women, and 10 percent of the tenured professors were women (Hensel, 1991, p. 1).

The entrance of women into colleges caused conflict. "It was widely believed that intellectual activity was contrary to feminine nature and harmful to women's health and reproductive capacity" (Chamberlain, 1988, p. 5). This was not merely a reflection of the 1800s; Harvard did not admit women to its medical school until 1945, its law school until 1950, and its business school until 1963. Yale and Princeton did not admit women undergraduates until 1969.

It is widely, and incorrectly, assumed that women have made steady increases in representation in the ranks of faculty and administration. According to Campus Trends, 1993 (El-Khawas, 1993, p. 20), campuses report that the greatest progress for women has been achieved among the student ranks, and that the "lowest ratings appear with respect to the representation of women among senior administrators, in senior faculty positions, and as members of boards of trustees."

Today women still face obstacles and resistance at every step of the education ladder, whether entering the hallowed halls of student life or the hallowed offices of the presidency. Gender discrimination continues to exist on college campuses but, like racism, is often subtle and systemic.

One type of conflict on campus that affects women more often than men is sexual harassment, although this problem has been strongly addressed in this decade. Nearly 90 percent of all institutions have policies on sexual harassment; some of those have been developed in this decade, whereas others have existed for many years (El-Khawas, 1993, p. 22; also see Riggs, Murrell, and Cutting, 1993).

A historical bastion of discrimination up until the 1970s, and still the subject of court battles in the 1990s, is athletics. While sex discrimination is prohibited in sports, inequality continues. Even in 1995, discrimination is being fought in the courts as universities fight legislation demanding equality for women in athletics.

Some of the newest conflicts on campus involve members of the gay, lesbian, and bisexual community. Attacks on students, faculty, and staff have increased as support and action groups have come out on campus. In D'Augelli's (1989, p. 317) study, nearly 75 percent of all lesbian and gay students in a university reported that they were the victims of discrimination, ranging from verbal abuse to threats of violence.

Increasing numbers of "others" on college campuses may be threatening to members of a majority group. "Thus, conflict may be intensified on many campuses as they become more diverse or more explicit in their efforts to diversify" (Smith, 1989, p. 60). For most colleges, that diversity has meant changes in the racial and ethnic composition of students, faculty, and staff. As Paula Brownlee, president of the Association of American Colleges and Universities, has noted, "Conflicts are now more observable, less suppressed on campuses because different groups have voices" (personal communication, March 22, 1995).

African Americans have been on college campuses for centuries. The first college specifically for African Americans was started before the Civil War. "The overwhelming majority opened after 1865 in response to two concerns: the need to quickly establish institutions to educate the newly freed slaves, and the segregationist sentiments of southern educators who opposed integrating blacks into already-existing white schools and colleges" (Wilson, 1994, p. xxv). Today there are 102 historically black colleges and universities in the United States. While some African Americans first attended the mixed-race institutions of Antioch, Oberlin, Franklin, and Rutland, most campuses were not open to blacks in the nineteenth century.

Racial conflict on campus continues. Boyer (1990) reported that 68 percent of the presidents of large research and doctoral institutions said that race relations are a problem on their campuses. Hurtado (1992) found that "one in four students at all four-year institutions and one in three at universities perceive considerable racial conflict."

Native Americans began their own educational system in 1815 when the "Five Civilized Tribes" joined forces. Few Native Americans found their way into other institutions of higher education during the nineteenth century (Cowley and Williams, 1991, p. 103). Native Americans have increased in numbers in higher education since 1981, but they are still underrepresented ("American Indians . . . ," 1995).

Because the first colleges in the Americas were founded by the Spanish at Santo Domingo in 1538, followed by universities in Mexico City and Lima in 1551, Chicanos have been involved in higher education for centuries. They began to participate in higher education in California as early as 1850. But in the United States they have always been underrepresented, both in the student body and in the faculty (Aguirre and Martinez, 1993).

In reference to Chicanos and Latinos in education, Cecilia Burciaga, an assistant dean at Stanford University, has spoken about the "adobe ceiling." "Unlike the glass ceiling that women and other minorities face, you can't see through it [the adobe] and it's made to last for centuries" (Rodriguez, 1994, p. 23).

Racial, ethnic, and gender discrimination is a significant element of the conflicts in higher education today. But this is not the only kind of conflict in higher education, as the content of this volume attests.

Is There More Conflict in the Academy Today?

Open discussion, free thought, and critical thinking—all hallmarks of the academy—also are precursors to conflict. And so conflict in institutions of higher education is inevitable.

Many higher education theorists suggest that economic issues are the most significant contributing factors to the problem because, with declining funds, no longer can the department subdivide when problems occur, no longer can money be the solution. "During the late 60s and early 70s, change always meant add on. There was less reason for conflict because your turf was not invaded. Resources were not involved. There was less threat of change. Now that is no longer the case" (Ernest Lynton, personal communication, April 26, 1995).

Unfortunately, a Catch 22 situation has developed. Fewer dollars are available to support the institutions, which causes more division, more animosity. That leads to a weak or negative campus climate, which leads to lower morale on campus, which leads to a weakening of the climate. And the cycle goes on. Malveaux (1994, p. 199) suggested that a shift in perceptions is the cause: "Perceptions of the academy have shifted from lofty 'ivory tower' to embattled economic unit."

Conflict in higher education is different today, and especially different from the 1960s era of conflict. Higher education consultant Parker Palmer (personal communication, March 14, 1995) has noted the change: "My sense is that conflict was associated with the hope of change in the 60s. There was the thought that conflict would make change—and it did. That is not true today. Today it is accompanied by cynicism, by the thought that nothing will change. Conflict has a bitter tone to it. Conflict is seen as a festering wound, not as reform or change. Now it is so internalized, especially in the faculty psyche, that it is interjected rather than energized as tools of reform. It is turned inward and creates rancor and distrust."

Robert Blackburn, editor of the *Journal of Higher Education,* agrees that more conflict exists today. "In higher education today there is a tenseness in the air; people are throwing bricks all the time. It is not as friendly a place. What is happening isn't organized revolt, but it isn't the way we remember it to be. The environment has changed, it isn't as supportive as individuals used to be" (personal communication, April 1995).

The climate on campus is not likely to get better as the decade progresses. As Clark Kerr (1990, p. 16), former president of the University of California, noted, "The 1990s will be another decade of major changes and conflicts."

Conflict has always existed in academia—from the marble walls of the Hellenic academy to the university of today. Conflict is now prevalent in every facet of the academy, and it is no longer hidden under the ivy.

References

American Association of University Professors. "Depression, Recovery, and Higher Education." In W. H. Cowley and D. Williams (eds.), *International and Historical Roots of American Higher Education.* New York: Garland, 1991.

Aguirre, A., Jr., and Martinez, R. O. *Chicanos in Higher Education: Issues and Dilemmas for the 21st Century.* ASHE-ERIC Higher Education Report No. 3. Washington, D.C.: George Washington University Press, 1993.

"American Indians/Alaska Natives Make Progress in Higher Education." *Higher Education and National Affairs,* 1995, *44* (10), 37–52.

Astin, A. W., Astin, H. S., Bayer, A. E., and Bisconti, A. S. *The Power of Protest.* San Francisco: Jossey-Bass, 1975.

Bishop, M. "Scholares Medii Aevi." *Horizon,* n.d., pp. 66–79.

Boyer, E. *Scholarship Reconsidered: Priorities of the Professoriate.* Princeton, N.J.: Carnegie Foundation for the Advancement of Teaching, 1990.

Califano, J. A., Jr. *The Student Revolution: A Global Confrontation.* New York: Norton, 1970.

Chamberlain, M. K. *Women in Academe: Progress and Prospects.* New York: Russell Sage Foundation, 1988.

Cowley, W. H., and Williams, D. (eds.). *International and Historical Roots of American Higher Education.* New York: Garland, 1991.

Cramer, F. "Why Did Roman Universities Fail?" *Harvard Educational Review,* 1939, *9,* 204–288.

D'Augelli, A. R. "Lesbians' and Gay Men's Experiences of Discrimination and Harassment in a University Community." *American Journal of Community Psychology,* 1989, *17* (3), 317–321.

El-Khawas, E. *Campus Trends, 1993.* Higher Education Panel Report No. 83. Washington, D.C.: American Council on Education, 1993.

Fulton, J. F., and Thompson, E. "Benjamin Silliman." In W. H. Cowley and D. Williams (eds.), *International and Historical Roots of American Higher Education.* New York: Garland, 1991.

Hensel, N. *Realizing Gender Equality in Higher Education: The Need to Integrate Work/Family Issues.* ASHE-ERIC Higher Education Report No. 2. Washington, D.C.: George Washington University Press, 1991.

Hurtado, S. "The Campus Racial Climate: Contexts of Conflict." *Journal of Higher Education,* 1992, *63* (5), 539–569.

Kant, I. *The Conflict of the Faculties.* (M. J. Gregor, trans.) New York: Abaris Books, 1979. (Originally published 1794.)

Kerr, C. "Higher Education Cannot Escape History: The 1990s." In L. W. Jones and F. A. Nowotny (eds.), *An Agenda for the New Decade.* New Directions for Higher Education, no. 70. San Francisco: Jossey-Bass, 1990.

Lewis, L. *Cold War on Campus: A Study of the Politics of Organizational Control.* New Brunswick: Transaction Books, 1988.

Malveaux, J. "Restructuring the Academy: 10 Years of Black Issues." *Black Issues in Higher Education,* 1994, *11* (4), 68.

Riggs, R. O., Murrell, P. H., and Cutting, J. *Sexual Harassment in Higher Education: From Conflict to Community.* ASHE-ERIC Higher Education Report No. 2. Washington, D.C.: Association for the Study of Higher Education, 1993.

Rodriguez, R. "Higher Education Crisis Looms for Chicanos/Latinos." *Black Issues in Higher Education,* 1994, *11* (3), 20–23.

Slosson, E. E. "The American Spirit in Education." In W. H. Cowley and D. Williams (eds.), *International and Historical Roots of American Higher Education.* New York: Garland, 1991. (Originally published 1921.)

Smith, D. G. *The Challenge of Diversity: Involvement or Alienation in the Academy.* ASHE-ERIC Higher Education Report No. 5. Washington, D.C.: George Washington University Press, 1989.

Wilson, R. *Black American Colleges and Universities: Profiles of Two-Year, Four-Year, and Professional Schools.* Detroit: Gale Research, 1994.

SUSAN A HOLTON *is professor of communication studies at Bridgewater State College, Bridgewater, Massachusetts, and director of the Massachusetts Faculty Development Consortium.*

Conflicts among faculty can be traced to the faculty enterprise; the format of their resolution is conditioned by the organizational culture of the institution.

From Collegiality to Confrontation: Faculty-to-Faculty Conflicts

Raymond R. Leal

The university has been an important setting for the development of conflict resolution systems for several decades. As academic communities have always been considered havens for all types of discourse and ideologies, it is natural that as centers of societal conflict they have been ideal settings for the establishment of these systems. Students, scholars, and administrators have all been involved in research, establishment of mediation programs, and development of new courses and degree programs aimed at the resolution of conflict in our society and on an international scale as well (Rule, 1993). It is clear, however, that the preponderance of mediation programs in academia are focused on student conflicts. The University of Hawaii and the University of Massachusetts at Amherst are generally recognized as the sites of the first mediation programs in the United States (Warters, 1991). Mediation on campuses is used in a variety of conflicts, including roommate problems, sexual harassment issues, racial and multicultural conflicts, and campus-community tensions (Rifkin, 1991). Universities have also adopted other conflict resolution processes, such as negotiation (Fisher and Ury, 1981) as well as the ombuds office concept (Rowe, 1991), in order to use less formal and costly mechanisms than litigation to resolve campus conflicts.

The informality and accessibility of student-based campus mediation programs have made them popular among students and have led to the growth of over one hundred such programs in America (Rifkin, 1991). While there are various models of these campus mediation programs (Leal, 1993), there is a shortage of either practice or research in the development of mediation programs that effectively deal with faculty disputes. This chapter is a brief, anecdotal exploration of such programs. I focus on the experiences of three

NEW DIRECTIONS FOR HIGHER EDUCATION, no. 92, Winter 1995   © Jossey-Bass Publishers

universities that have attempted to use conflict resolution processes as informal dispute resolution mechanisms on their campuses. Attention is devoted to the conditions that led these universities to change the ways in which faculty disputes were handled within their organizational cultures. Additionally, I compare these three universities' approaches to conflict resolution and discuss the advancement of the notion that mediation in particular is quite amenable for use in the resolution of faculty disputes. The ensuing discussion relies on the basic premise that the single most important factor in the adoption of conflict resolution processes by faculty in an American university is the organizational culture of the institution.

Prior to any discussion of faculty initiatives for conflict resolution, one must have a preliminary understanding of the faculty enterprise in academia, current and future tensions facing universities, and the impact of organizational culture on the design of conflict resolution systems in universities. American academe has for some time endorsed the collegial model of decision making, which requires knowledge of the consensus-building process. Many faculty members refer to one another as colleagues, and to outsiders it appears that a university is a "government by committee" characterized by a faculty who exercises great autonomy (Getman, 1992). This omnipotent view of American faculty is belied by certain incongruities often overlooked by outsiders. Does the academy prepare its doctorates to live in a community marked by consensus building as a way of business?

The Faculty Enterprise

Membership into the academy requires certain rites of passage through which most doctorate students must journey prior to their acceptance as regular members in good standing. The indoctrination of faculty entails full knowledge and understanding of respective disciplinary paradigms, conceptual language and formulas, relevant disciplinary literature, and appropriate research methodologies. A part of the ritual—continued in greater intensity throughout an academic career for many—is the ability to withstand the criticism of colleagues in open discussion, usually at professional presentations, as well as the ability to confront colleagues regarding the shortcomings of their research. In many instances this makes for the development of individuals who welcome confrontation and collegial conflict. This developmental experience leads to incongruity for faculty members, who must operate in a collegial atmosphere. As most faculty members are not trained in the communication and conflict resolution processes of problem solving, consensus building, negotiation, and mediation, their effectiveness as participants in a collegial, consensus-building environment may be limited, with outcomes that are unproductive for the university.

This value incongruity between confrontation and collegiality may have serious consequences for the operation of a university, whose administration is usually focused on maintaining harmony among all its constituents. There are various ways in which faculty-to-faculty conflicts become problematic for colleagues, departments, schools, universities, and professional associations. At the department level, some of the points that can lead to confrontation among colleagues include the manner in which department meetings are conducted, ideological differences among faculty, ideological direction of the department, class scheduling, compensatory time for certain faculty members, allocation of resources and office space, and promotions, to name but a few.

The normal channel followed by a dissatisfied faculty member is to meet with the appropriate dean to seek redress, or to continue through university administrative channels until the faculty member receives satisfaction. Usually, the faculty member's last recourses are to file a formal grievance or to pursue litigation. The resolution of a faculty member's concerns can easily become a conflict that requires time, energy, and financial resources for the university. Unfortunately, the faculty member's dissatisfaction can also lead to open confrontation with colleagues and the use of a variety of techniques by the aggrieved faculty member to suspend the collegial model until the conflict is resolved.

On a more systemic level, faculty-to-faculty conflicts can transcend department lines and become conflicts between departments or between schools in a university. The net results of all these faculty conflicts are faculty and staff stress, a loss of productivity, an inability to effectively meet students' needs, and a drain on the university's administrative resources. Formal grievance procedures and litigation are costly enterprises and often leave the disputants feeling less valued by their colleagues and the university.

Additional sources of conflict for universities today include budgetary reductions, calls for more public accountability, decreasing enrollments, rapid technological changes in pedagogy, demands for cultural diversity, recent judicial opinions weakening affirmative action initiatives, and changing demographics of college students. Getman (1992) has more specifically outlined the conflicts and tensions in academia, which include the conflict between teaching and research, challenges to academic freedom, the struggle over multiculturalism, and the impact of minority and feminist activism. Getman's *In the Company of Scholars: The Struggle for the Soul of Higher Education* provides keen insights into the current organizational values dominant in American universities and clearly delineates the conflicts in academia that must be resolved if American higher education is to remain a viable and creative enterprise.

From Conflict to Collegiality

How then is one to redirect colleagues back to the collegial model of the academic enterprise? Can conflict resolution offer a bridge back to the academy's collegial model and provide an alternative way to deal with the modern-day stresses placed on university faculty members? It is a hopeful development that several universities are now moving forward with the implementation of faculty-to-faculty dispute resolution systems. In this section, I detail the efforts of a major research university, a medium-size public university, and a small private university to develop more collegial environments on their campuses.

Perhaps the most fundamental consideration for a conflict resolution design consultant working with university systems is to gain, first, an appreciation of the organizational culture of the university seeking to implement a faculty-to-faculty conflict resolution program. How are the faculty affected by the university's mission, goals, long-term plans, setting, and faculty and student body demographics? Does the leadership of the university have an interest in empowering its faculty members to resolve their own conflicts (Murphy, 1993)? Who at the university will act as an advocate for conflict resolution and who will provide financial support for its development on campus? How will conflict resolution processes affect established grievance procedures? What type of university is it and what are the faculty behaviors rewarded by the administration? What is likely to be the relation among conflict resolution processes and the faculty governance body, the faculty union, and the faculty contract?

What follows is a description of three universities' efforts to incorporate faculty-to-faculty conflict resolution systems on their campuses. The first case involves a major research university in a rural setting that, through its faculty welfare committee and the leadership of several faculty members, decided to procure the services of a national training consultant to train selected faculty in the process of mediation. The impetus for the use of mediation as a dispute resolution process among faculty came from an elaborate and very time-consuming grievance procedure that generally left faculty members dissatisfied. It is noteworthy that faculty members chose to learn mediation because they saw it as the most informal alternative dispute resolution process and one in which they would have more control than administrators. These reasons reinforce previous research on why people choose to use mediation over more formal conflict resolution processes (Tyler, 1990).

When questioned about the need for a conflict resolution process such as the ombuds concept to deal with power imbalances between faculty and administrators, the faculty members indicated that if conflicts among and between faculty members were resolved more appropriately, the need for involving administrators in faculty members' conflicts would be greatly minimized. They also pointed to the confidentiality of the mediation process as advantageous, since most of them preferred that their conflicts not reach the deans' offices. Several faculty members emphasized that they thought a mediation system would help with faculty-staff conflicts in the future, but their primary concern in the first year would be to develop and institutionalize a faculty mediation system on campus that worked and was respected by all members of the university community.

The second case study involves a medium-size public university in an urban setting whose student body was largely composed of commuters. Over the years the organizational structure of the university had led to conflicts between the administrators and faculty regarding jurisdiction and decision-making authority. Another point for consideration was that spatially the university was designed in such a way as to limit interaction among its employees, which impacted on the informal communication system of the university. Much university business was conducted by paperwork. Many of the university's grievance procedures resided in the administrative vice president's office, so it was not surprising that the impetus for a conflict resolution system came from this office in an effort to improve communications between administrators and faculty.

While both middle-level and high-level administrators and faculty were invited to attend the initial mediation training, those trained were largely middle-level administrators and a few faculty members. The participants were enthusiastic about their training and the potential benefits of a mediation program on campus and took an interesting perspective in the design of their conflict resolution system. It was decided that most conflicts on campus were the result of either miscommunication or lack of information. Several participants indicated that the spatial, user-unfriendly atmosphere of the university was part of the problem and that in many cases mediation would not be needed once the employee was given the needed information. This notion was instrumental in the development of a three-level conflict resolution system. The first level involved the designation of the trained participants as problem solvers, who in addition to receiving mediation training were then extensively trained in the procedures and operations of the university. These problem solvers were clearly identified by a distinctive identification label outside each of their offices and were located in every school of the university.

The second level of the system involved a referral by the problem solver to the administrative vice president's office where the coordinator for the system would appoint a mediator to deal with conflicts among employees, whether staff or faculty. Many of the initial mediations were among staff members, indicating some hesitancy by faculty members to use the system, perhaps since it was a conflict resolution system initiated by the administration and not the faculty. So far, the general impression among faculty members on campus is that communications have improved and that faculty are more respected than in the past. This observation points to a need for an in-depth survey of faculty members regarding the resolution of conflicts on their campus.

As many of the past conflicts between administrators and faculty had resulted in litigation and many faculty members viewed the balance of power in favor of the administration, the training participants saw the need for a third level in their system. The Ombuds Office was thus established to deal with higher-level conflicts on campus, where power imbalances might affect outcomes. There were several discussions on how to properly structure this third level in the system and on how much autonomy was needed for this office to be useful in the university's conflict resolution system. For reasons unknown, this level of the university's system has been the least developed or used by the administration as an alternative to litigation.

The third case study involves a small private university located in an urban setting and noted for its liberal arts education. The organizational culture of the university emphasizes informality and relative autonomy for its faculty, with a very strong student development office. Both faculty and staff are encouraged to develop close and nurturing interactions with students. Additionally, many faculty members view themselves as conciliators because of how closely they work with students during their academic careers. The initial impetus for mediation training on campus came from the Dean of Students Office in an effort to better prepare residential counselors to interact with dormitory residents. The initial training was conducted by a campus faculty member who had instituted mediation training in one of the university's academic departments and was a national conflict resolution training consultant.

The approach taken by faculty on this campus to learn about and use conflict resolution closely followed the organizational culture of informality and autonomy. One faculty member, the training consultant, was queried by two other faculty members, who were then sent to a national demonstration project involving mediation in higher education. This experience led to their further involvement in conflict resolution when they both attended national mediation training seminars. These faculty members used their newly acquired skills in a disciplinary fashion—one applying them to public education and the other to public policy issues involving the environment. Further discussions with other faculty members led one of the university's vice presidents, also a faculty member, to undergo a national mediation training seminar with a focus on using these skills in dealing with faculty on campus.

This diffusion of mediation training among faculty led to its use in daily interactions by these faculty members with their peers and students. While there have not been any formal faculty mediations on campus, the interest that mediation has engendered has led to its inclusion in a revised faculty handbook, which may lead to its further adoption by other faculty members over time. One interesting note is that the directors of key administrative offices on campus have called on faculty members trained as mediators to assist them in the training of their staffs, which is a reversal of the situation mentioned in the case study. So, the development of a faculty conflict resolution system on this campus has progressed informally even though there is an established student mediation center on campus and several community outreach initiatives dealing with mediation in the public schools.

Conclusion

What can be learned from these three case studies, however anecdotal the findings? First, all three universities' programs continue to develop and expand. Two of the three universities' programs were initiated by faculty members, one by an important segment of the faculty governance body and one by an individual faculty member. The organizational culture of each university affected the design of each model. The university with a large research faculty was easily able to gain support for its program and focus specifically on faculty disputes. The university with a strong administrative structure pushed for its program in an effort to improve communications between administrators and faculty. The small, informal university approached mediation in a much more informal and autonomous way than did the other two universities.

In spite of these three different approaches, all three institutions have been successful with conflict resolution in various ways. What is clear from these experiences is that there is no one model uniquely suited to the development of conflict resolution systems on university campuses. The development of these three approaches to collegiate conflict resolution has largely been tied to the organizational culture of each university. Perhaps the greatest lesson of the experiences described here is that in order to design a successful conflict resolution system on a university campus, one must first learn the particular culture of the university as it will affect whether or not a system is adopted by faculty members. Conflict resolution trainers must be culturally literate about the various forms in which universities are configured. Mediation training in a university setting is a process in search of a culture, and so no one model is appropriate for all universities. Last, it does appear that some faculty members see conflict resolution processes, particularly mediation, as a way to return to the collegial model of the university.

References

Fisher, R., and Ury, W. *Getting to Yes: Negotiating Agreement Without Giving In.* Boston: Houghton Mifflin, 1981.

Getman, J. *In the Company of Scholars: The Struggle for the Soul of Higher Education.* Austin: University of Texas Press, 1992.

Leal, R. "The Next Generation of Campus Mediation Programs." Paper presented at the Society for Professionals in Dispute Resolution Regional Conference, San Antonio, Texas, August 1993.

Murphy, E. C. *The Genius of Sitting Bull.* Englewood Cliffs, N.J.: Prentice Hall, 1993.

Rifkin, J. "An Overview of Dispute Resolution in Educational Institutions." *NIDR Forum,* Spring 1991, pp. 1–4.

Rowe, M. P. "The Ombudsman Role in a Dispute Resolution System." *Negotiation Journal,* Oct. 1991, pp. 353–362.

Rule, C. "The Planning and Design of a Student Centered Collegiate Conflict Management System." Unpublished senior thesis, Haverford College, 1993.

Tyler, T. *Why People Obey the Law.* New Haven, Conn.: Yale University Press, 1990.

Warters, B. "Mediation on Campus: A History and Planning Guide." *The Fourth R: Newsletter of the National Association of Mediation in Education,* 1991, 33, 4–5.

RAYMOND R. LEAL *is chair of and associate professor in the Public Justice Department at Saint Mary's University, San Antonio, Texas.*

Conflict abounds in student life, where economic stress,
close living conditions, and exposure to new people and
new ideas challenge students.

"Can't We Settle This?"
Student Conflicts in Higher Education
and Options for Resolution

Jacqueline Gibson

The pressures of college and university life generate abundant conflict among students. Students' exposure to academic stress, frequent challenges to their beliefs, fatigue, shared living quarters, and other trying facets of campus culture make interpersonal and group conflict an inevitable part of student life.

Interpersonal, intragroup, and intergroup conflict is best defined as "an expressed struggle between at least two interdependent parties who perceive incompatible goals, scarce resources, and interference from others in achieving their goals" (Hocker and Wilmot, 1994, p. 21). Like others in conflict, students find themselves in opposition over goals and needs, and in competition over scarce resources. Students struggle over romantic relationships, roommate relationships, disagreements with instructors, ideological differences within organizations—a multitude of situations. Moreover, students' relative naïveté often serves to muddy issues and intensify emotional costs.

Options for managing or resolving conflicts faced by students range from choosing to do nothing at all to taking legal action. Increasingly, campus programs and services are offering students the option of assistance or intervention from neutral third parties, who function under various guises and configurations. They can be found in administration buildings, in counseling or advising centers, in offices staffed by students, in legal services or judicial affairs offices, and in the person of the dean of students. Campus administrators and student leaders recognize that mediation and conflict resolution services can manage or resolve student conflicts before they escalate into fiscally and emotionally costly formal or legal proceedings.

NEW DIRECTIONS FOR HIGHER EDUCATION, no. 92, Winter 1995 © Jossey-Bass Publishers

27

A structured mediation service for students is generally visible in one of three forms: peer mediation, a campus mediator or mediation office, and mediation offered by student affairs personnel. Because peer mediation is increasingly common from middle school onward, entering college students may expect to find this service available.

Student affairs professionals are often assigned conflict resolution responsibilities without the necessary training to provide effective arbitration and mediation. Training of existing personnel and the support of new dispute resolution programs can satisfy the urgent needs for such expertise. Mediation particularly appeals to both students and administrators dissatisfied with the overly formal and legalistic procedures developed to ensure due process. Students find that sitting down to talk things out, with someone to help facilitate that process, brings about both an intellectual and an emotional satisfaction impossible through other means.

Student affairs professionals can prepare for their roles as dispute resolution facilitators by becoming familiar with the range of conflicts that students encounter. The following vignettes represent a few typical student conflicts, each followed by a range of options the students may have available, and a brief look at the possible consequences of each option.

Roommate Relationships

Roommate conflict is one of the most common experiences college students share. Accustomed to eighteen years of family life, often with their own private bedrooms, students find themselves in a residence hall, on a floor with thirty others, and sharing a small living space with one or more strangers. The help students do or do not receive and the measure of success they have in resolving roommate conflicts can impact their approaches to future conflicts and can increase their understanding of the responsibilities inherent to roommate and other interdependent relationships.

Karen and Shawna, university residents and roommates, complain about each other to their resident assistant (RA), Beth. Karen complains that Shawna often borrows her clothes without asking and says that she does not know how to get Shawna to stop. Shawna complains that Karen keeps her up at night by coming in late, often with a group of friends who talk and laugh loudly, seemingly unaware or unconcerned that Shawna is trying to sleep.

Options and consequences: By discussing the problem with the RA, Karen and Shawna have each attempted to begin finding a solution. Meanwhile, both are avoiding a logical option: simply addressing each other and talking it out. Being unskilled in assertiveness techniques, they may not know what to do, or they may fear mishandling the situation. However, if they continue to avoid this confrontation, friction and discomfort undoubtedly will increase until hostility erupts. At this point, they have several options, each involving different possible consequences.

First, if they will come together to talk things out with Beth, they might reach an agreement to adapt their behaviors to satisfy the other. Possible consequences include (1) a recommitment to live together peacefully in friendly roommate fashion, (2) simple agreements to ask before borrowing and to schedule late night socials, and (3) increased confidence in Beth as a fair and helpful third party.

Second, if reluctant to talk it out with Beth, they may be willing to seek a more formal solution with a peer or professional mediator on campus. Possible consequences include (1) a simple understanding that one's behavior offends the other; (2) a more detailed solution, including a written and signed agreement about hours, noise, borrowing, expectations, and other roommate issues; and (3) satisfaction derived from exercising responsibility by asking for assistance and solving their own problems.

Third, if they are not willing to talk it out between themselves or with a third party, one of them might ask to be moved to another room. Possible consequences include (1) a move, as determined by the availability of another room and the institution's policy; (2) a short- or long-range period of coolness, probably resulting in permanent damage to the relationship; and (3) either roommate's learning about constructively solving problems arising from conflict with roommates, friends, and intimates.

Workplace Relationships Among Students

Although the setting in the following vignette is the residence hall, the conflict could just as easily occur between lab assistants, food service workers, or other student co-workers.

Lianne and Mark are RAs on the same floor of a coed residence hall. Their jobs require close cooperation, regular communication, and joint decision making. By midyear, however, Lianne decides that Mark is incompetent. She stops consulting him about problems on the floor and tells several people that she considers him "worthless." She rarely talks with him, notifying him of decisions after she has made them and increasingly distancing herself from him. Her behavior puzzles Mark. He understands that she does not think he is as skilled as her, but he believes that he is working hard to ensure that the floor residents like and respect him. Chang, the resident director, knows about the situation and worries that the floor will not run smoothly, that students may take sides with Lianne and Mark, possibly along gender lines, and that conflict will characterize the floor. Lianne asks Chang to do an early performance appraisal and fire Mark for incompetence. Mark suggests that Chang reassign Lianne and bring in another female RA to replace her. Instead, Chang asks them both to settle their conflict by talking. He suggests the following options: talk it out one-on-one, talk it out with Chang in his office, or go to the campus mediation center for help working it out.

Options and consequences: First, if Lianne and Mark talk this out one-on-one, then (1) Lianne might compound the problem by simply venting her frustration and taking a blaming approach or (2) they might be able to sort out their differences and come up with an agreement about how to work together more effectively, but only if they are skilled communicators and hold their working relationship in high priority. As a well-trained professional, Chang is unlikely to cave in to either RA's demands, either to reassign Lianne or to reevaluate Mark; instead, he is more likely to direct them to address the issue squarely.

Second, if Chang conducts this conversation and directs them to work it out, then Lianne and Mark might (1) vent their anger and frustration and reluctantly agree to find ways to work together, probably with less contact; (2) recognize that they are stuck working together and follow Chang's directions about how to avoid problems in the future; or (3) recommit to a solid working relationship and meet regularly with Chang to discuss their progress.

Third, if Lianne and Mark take their problem to the campus mediation center or to the counseling center, where they are not under the watchful eye of their employer, they are more likely to state their real desires, and to take greater responsibility for settling the issue. (1) Lianne might admit she just does not want to work with Mark at all and refuse to cooperate, leaving the mediator to return the case to Chang for his decision or (2) Lianne and Mark might commit to trying to work it out, in which case the mediator or counselor can help them explore ways to carefully identify the problem issues, seek options for solutions, and continue to work toward a cooperative relationship.

Broken Relationships Between Intimate Partners

Broken romantic relationships, short-term or long-term, affect student life significantly, interrupting students' study habits, concentration, and sense of security. Except for counseling, students rarely seek help except from their friends and families. Students may seek help from a trusted friend, a RA, or a campus minister when a dating relationship dissolves. For more complex relationships, some campuses have alternatives, such as professional mediators who handle divorce, postdivorce, and divorcelike cases for students. The following vignette illustrates such alternatives and shows how campus services can facilitate retention in these cases.

Jason and Sumiko have been unmarried partners for four years and have a two-year-old daughter, Amelia. Jason graduates within the year. Sumiko has been attending part-time and is about to declare her major. Sumiko, who never wanted to marry, now wants to end the intimate part of the relationship. Jason is struggling to save the relationship. He fails to understand why Sumiko, mother of his child, wants to end their family status. Sumiko wants to remain friends and coparents with Jason, yet free herself of the expectations of romantic partnership. Their academic work suffers while they attempt to maintain a family life because they feel that Amelia's need for attention and reassurance takes precedence over their studies.

Options and consequences: Sumiko and Jason have talked endlessly about resolving this issue but are not getting past the dilemma. Both fear losing time with Amelia. Also, they know that living apart will cost more than living together; both fear not being able to afford school. Services likely to help them include student legal assistance, the counseling center, and the mediation center.

First, if they choose a legal route to determine custody of their daughter and to divide their few minor possessions, these are possible consequences: (1) They may be turned away, as campus legal services vary; some do not handle divorces, and others cannot represent one student against another; (2) the circumstances may require them to hire attorneys, an expense they can scarcely afford; or (3) they may find themselves moving away from cooperation and toward competition, since the intrinsic structure of the legal system puts disputing parties into an adversarial relationship.

Second, if they go to the counseling center, (1) Jason's desire to maintain the intimate relationship and Sumiko's desire for change will be addressed immediately, and both will receive emotional support; (2) Jason might come to understand Sumiko's desire for change; (3) Sumiko might change her mind and decide to remain Jason's intimate partner; or (4) if they decide on a permanent separation, the counselor might not be able to help them work through the practical matters of joint parenting and child support.

Third, if they seek help from the mediation center, (1) the mediation strategy of seeking common ground will help them to focus on their concern for their daughter; (2) because the mediation process weighs their relationship as much as the outcome, they will focus on developing a coparenting process that will benefit all three; and (3) the clarity and bindingness of their cooperative agreement will provide both emotional and practical satisfaction.

Sexual Harassment

Sexual harassment on campus is "unwanted sexual attention that makes a person uncomfortable or causes problems in school, work, or social settings" (University of Oregon, 1993, p. 1). In order to solve the problem, unequal power between the contending parties must be balanced somehow, whether through formal grievance processes or through a third-party neutral who can back the university's formal policies while guiding the parties toward understanding and agreement. If a sexual harassment case is routed improperly, gossip, publicity, ruined reputations, and lack of real consequences may result in a crisis of fear and frustration for one or both students. School officials often underestimate the potential for damage in student-versus-student sexual harassment cases; the superficially equal status of the two students blinds observers to the power imbalance created by gender, size, strength, and culture. Also, few student-to-student sexual harassment cases are reported. The following vignette illustrates how the power imbalance impacts the effectiveness of various options for resolution.

Naomi and Josh work together as volunteer coordinators for a campus program that links student volunteers with various community agencies. They have become increasingly good friends over the past two years and worked well together until an incident changed things between them. At work one day, they were talking in a friendly fashion, and when another male worker joined them, the talking led to teasing. As the men engaged in a play of one-upsmanship, the teasing led to sexual remarks demeaning women, particularly Naomi. Although Naomi asked the men to stop, Josh did not, and eventually he made a remark about being able to "get what he wanted from her, even if she pretended to resist," which made Naomi angry and, to her surprise, afraid.

When Naomi told Margaret, the program director, about the incident, Margaret declared Josh's behavior "abominable" and wanted something done immediately. Other students who heard about the incident divided into two camps: one sided with Naomi and wanted Josh to resign, the other sided with Josh and accused Naomi of overreacting. Josh defended his words as teasing, denying any intention of harassment. Naomi withdrew, even from friends, found herself frightened of being alone with Josh or other men, and reacted angrily to those who took the incident lightly.

Options and consequences: First, if her campus has a procedure for such cases, Naomi might file a formal grievance with the appropriate office on her campus. An investigation would ensue, including interviews and fact finding that would lead to a judicial board hearing, resulting either in exoneration of Josh or in a statement of wrongdoing and consequent punitive action. Depending on the degree of confidentiality with which the procedure is conducted, which differs from campus to campus, the investigation could produce various drastic effects. On one hand, a school or community newspaper might publish the story. On the other, confidentiality measures may prevent the victim from ever learning the outcome of the proceedings. These outcomes generate new possible consequences. (1) If Naomi is not allowed to hear the outcome, she may feel further weakened by the system; (2) if Josh is punished, Naomi may feel vindicated and strengthened; (3) Josh may resent the damage to his reputation, become estranged from Naomi, and remain uncertain about exactly what he did wrong; (4) the two will be unlikely to resume their friendship; (5) Naomi and Josh will find working together intolerable, and one may feel pressured to resign from his or her position; and (6) friends and co-workers may continue to gossip, taking sides and continuing the dispute.

Second, if Naomi does not know where to seek help, Margaret may intervene as arbitrator. Possible consequences include (1) Margaret setting strict guidelines for future workplace contact between Naomi and Josh; (2) further discomfort in the workplace and resignation of one or both parties; (3) Naomi's fear that uncomfortable language and threatening circumstances may occur in the workplace again; (4) Josh never understanding why his remarks scared Naomi; (5) gossip and divisive side taking among co-workers; and (6) problem-solving talks within the organization to define correct behavior among co-workers and procedures for handling sexual harassment.

Third, Naomi has two conflicting goals in this case. She feels threatened enough that she wants institutional support; she also wants Josh to understand the damage he has done. She continues to regret the loss of their friendship. If she can talk to Josh with a campus mediator present, who will value her investment in the friendship and provide an alternative to disengagement while simultaneously representing the authority and protective power of the institution, both her goals may be satisfied. Some possible consequences of handling the grievance informally with a campus mediator or ombudsperson include (1) Naomi feeling safe and confident enough in the setting to clearly describe Josh's actions and her resulting feelings; (2) Josh's defensiveness being reduced by the facilitated one-on-one discussion, so that he really hears Naomi's concerns; and (3) the two parties having the opportunity to make agreements that will probably lead to increased trust and possibly renew the friendship (for instance, they might attend a rape prevention class or workshop together, or arrange one for all the workers and volunteers in their agency, both strengthening their friendship and providing a positive outcome for the group).

Conclusion

The previous conflict vignettes present typical student conflicts; however, lack of space requires omission of other types equally familiar to faculty and student affairs professionals. Other common conflicts include (1) fights between groups of young men, such as athletes and fraternity members; (2) racial harassment between Euro-American students and students of color; (3) off-campus roommates struggling to get the slacker roommate to do his or her share of the work or pay for the groceries; (4) former romantic partners who have to work together, or whose friends are still friends; (5) the student body president and vice president in conflict about communication over goals for the year; and (6) members of a campus cultural or political group in conflicting subgroups, divided over programming goals.

With the many pressures now on students—academic, economic, ethical, and cultural—it is no wonder that they are beset by conflicts they have little skill in resolving. Colleges and universities must ensure that they can provide competent services for students to manage those struggles so that they can complete their expensive and complex educations. As the twenty-first century approaches, campuses must address the issue of how to achieve peaceable, long-term resolution of conflicts.

Managing such conflicts is critical to retention, but it also is critical to student success in achieving personal and career goals. Alternate dispute resolution programs are not expensive, and they save schools money by deterring the lawsuits that students occasionally file when they become overly frustrated. Campus dispute resolution programs can serve two major objectives: to keep students in school and to teach them valuable, life-long conflict management skills.

To ensure that their schools are adequately equipped to deal with student conflict, administrators should examine their structural and human resources to determine how best to implement appropriate programs. Students should look at the alternatives available to them to see what conflict management resources might aid them in completing their educations. As our world becomes more divisive and more complex, campuses need to build in mechanisms to bring people together peaceably, to teach communication skills for effectively resolving conflict, and to uphold the principles of cooperation and collaboration in everyday life.

References

Hocker, J. L., and Wilmot, W. W. *Interpersonal Conflict.* (4th ed.) Madison, Wis.: Brown & Benchmark, 1994.

University of Oregon. *Sexual Harassment: A Guide for University of Oregon Students.* Eugene: Offices of the Dean of Students, Affirmative Action, Student Advocacy, International Education and Exchange, and Unwanted Sexual Behavior Task Force, University of Oregon, 1993.

JACQUELINE GIBSON is director of the mediation program at the University of Oregon, Eugene, and is a member of the Higher Education Committee of the National Association for Mediation in Education.

Department chairs experience conflict from three main aspects of their role: institutional, interpersonal, and positional.

Department Chairs Under Siege: Resolving the Web of Conflict

Walter H. Gmelch

When one thinks of conflict, what is the first word that comes to mind? Most chairs develop images of controversy, disagreement, or differing opinions among faculty members. While negative images of conflict may predominate, is controversy necessarily undesirable? Emotional responses to conflict may be positive (excitement, enjoyment, stimulation, curiosity, creativity, commitment, involvement), negative (anger, distrust, resentment, fear, rejection), or even neutral (change or a different point of view). Conflict can have both positive and negative effects on departments as well as faculty and department chairs. In a positive way, conflict helps define issues, resolve issues, increase group cohesion, establish alliances with other groups, and keep faculty alert to one anothers' interests. However, if not managed properly, conflict can also increase faculty antagonism, lead to interdepartment tension, disrupt normal channels of communication, and divert faculty's attention from a department's goals and mission.

This chapter addresses the three main themes of department chair conflict: conflict inherent to the structure of higher education (*institutional*), conflict created when people work together (*interpersonal*), and conflict woven into the role of the chair position (*positional*). These three concentric circles of conflict create the department chair's web of tension.

Institutional Influence of Department Conflict

The first step a chair must take toward a positive and constructive conflict style is to recognize the nature and causes of conflict in the department and the university or college. Several institutional models of universities have emerged from which to view the cracks in the ivory tower, specifically, the bureaucratic, political, collegial, and anarchical institutional perspectives (Baldridge, 1971; Birnbaum, 1988). First, observed from the *bureaucratic* model, one assumes conflict will occur but could be controlled through bureaucratic roles or procedures. The *political* model accepts conflict as a normal part of academic life emanating from conflicting interests between and among individuals and groups of faculty. The *collegial* model of university governance views the academy as a "community of scholars" where conflict is abnormal, necessitating its elimination through deliberation and reason. Finally, *anarchical* institutions exhibit three characteristics: problematic goals, unclear technology, and fluid participation. Such institutions flourish in conditions of abundant resources and decline with reduced resources forcing difficult choices and increased conflict. While all four models represent abstractions of reality, they do allow academics to understand and, to some extent, predict the type of conflict each of the systems represents. The use of alternative models from which to view conflict leads to differing, yet complementary, perceptions of the cracks in the ivory tower within the departments.

A review of the research on organizational conflict reveals how one creates and manages conflict in each of these models. Higher education institutions are potentially plagued with conflict due to their many levels, rules and regulations, specialized disciplines, segmented rewards, autonomy, and high interdependence. It is important for department chairs to recognize how to view the inherent conflict from each institutional model. They must understand and recognize the barriers to productive departments built into the structure of institutions of higher education. As chairs, they need to realize that regardless of the causes, it is their responsibility to confront these barriers in order to patch the cracks in the ivory tower.

Bureaucratic Model: Structure and Specialization. As the size of an organization increases, goals become less clear, interpersonal relationships become more formal, departments become more specialized, and the potential for conflict intensifies. As the administrative line-authority in universities increases, the potential for conflict across the echelons also increases. Thus, chairs must strive to flatten the hierarchy for better communication and increased autonomy.

Also, high degrees of specialization increase the intensity of conflict (Corwin, 1969; Robbins, 1974). Disciplines in higher education segmented into departments suffer more conflict than, for example, homogeneous elementary schools. Academic departments, housed in separate buildings, experience more conflict than organizations with less specialization and fragmentation. This, of course, does not presuppose that elementary schools represent a more positive working environment than colleges; conflict can also cause positive outcomes. Nevertheless, chairs need to use the creative conflict from specializations to broaden the vision within each discipline.

Political Model. Political scientists suggest five bases of social power (French and Raven, 1968). In essence, department chairs can influence faculty through several sources: the authority vested in the position (legitimate power), their ability to provide rewards and recognition (reward power) or to provide punishment and withhold rewards (coercive power), their knowledge and skills (expertise power), and their personal persuasion (referent power). Universities and colleges rely predominantly on symbols rather than coercion or financial reward to influence employees. Department chairs typically use formal control by virtue of both their personalities and positions to motivate and coordinate their colleagues (Etzioni, 1964). But where power is excessive, chairs can expect it to be challenged by faculty, causing increased conflict. Faculty hold exceptional power due to their professionalism—their expertise. Chairs must recognize these sources of power and use them wisely.

Rewards and recognition also contribute significantly to conflict. When a differential reward structure is used for two or more groups or departments, conflict is likely to occur. In other words, the more that rewards emphasize separate performance rather than combined performance, the greater the conflict. This is even more prevalent if faculty perceive they are competing for the same or limited resources. If chairs must divide a fixed sum of merit increases among faculty, they will likely encounter conflict between and among colleagues.

Collegial Model: Community of Scholars. In much the same way that differentiated rewards and recognition create conflict, the more that faculty must rely on one another, or one department relies on another department, or one academic course builds on another to complete a task or gain achievement, the more that conflict will increase. A limited amount of resources to be shared among colleagues sets the stage for increased conflict. When one faculty member's gain is another's loss, faculty believe that the allocation of resources is a zero-sum game, and the department is destined for conflict. In his definitive work on conflict, sociologist Georg Simmel (1955) concluded that conflict will occur when the activities of one group have a direct consequence on another group's ability to achieve its goal. Therefore, building a community of scholars will necessitate faculty interdependence and result in tension among faculty as they become dependent on one another to achieve the desired results.

Anarchical Model: Faculty Autonomy. "Imagine that you're either the referee, coach, player, or spectator at an unconventional soccer match: the field for the game is round; there are several goals scattered haphazardly around the circular field; people can enter and leave the game whenever they want to; they can throw balls in whenever they want . . . and the game is played as if it makes sense" (James March, in Weick, 1976, p. 1). This analogy may resonate a note for department chairs and faculty where, in a chaotic manner, faculty can do what they want. It resembles an organized anarchy, an institutional oxymoron as coined by Cohen and March (1974). In anarchical institutions of higher education, where faculty have a great deal of autonomy, the potential for *inter*personal conflict increases since roles and expectations become less clear and more difficult to monitor and supervise. On the flip side, this autonomy also reduces faculty's potential *intra*personal conflict. The key is to capture the energy from autonomy and synergistically transform it into productive ideas for the department.

In summary, the four models of universities and colleges reveal institutional relationships that increase the intensity of conflict for department chairs: more perceived levels of authority in the hierarchy, greater rules and regulations, higher degrees of specialization, increased use of positional power over personal power, greater differences in rewards and recognition, and greater independence and competition for limited resources. It is not difficult to infer that higher education institutions are potentially plagued with conflict due to their many levels, rules and regulations, specialized disciplines, segmented rewards, high interdependence, and use of authoritative power.

These four models serve as conceptual lenses that focus our attention on the conflict inherent to higher education. Unfortunately, many department chairs view institutional conflict from a personal filter and believe that if they are involved in controversy, it must be due to their personalities. However, even though chairs may not like to talk about conflict, they need to accept the idea that it occurs and will be inevitable due to how colleges and universities work.

Interpersonal Influence of Department Conflict

Chairs suffer from more interpersonal conflict among their colleagues than with their deans or students. This fact is reconfirmed by a study conducted by the Center for the Study of the Department Chair that found that chairs identified conflict with colleagues as their major source of stress (Gmelch, Carroll, Seedorf, and Wentz, 1990). For example, over 40 percent of eight hundred department chairs suffered excessive stress from making decisions affecting others, resolving collegial differences, and evaluating faculty performance. In contrast, only 17 percent of the chairs complained of excessive stress from resolving differences with deans, and 5 percent with students.

In the same study, chairs also described when they felt most dissatisfied with their jobs. Second only to bureaucratic red tape and paperwork were the chairs' frustration with interpersonal conflict. Overall, 60 percent of their dissatisfaction came from dealing with faculty colleagues, from the following sources of faculty conflict: (1) *Interfaculty conflict:* Most of the chairs' dissatisfaction came from faculty disagreeing with one another, which resulted in "bickering, whining, and feuding," "acting without reason," and "ideological and personal wars." (2) *Faculty attitude:* Chairs felt disappointed when faculty were seen as "unimaginative, apathetic, disengaged" colleagues, who "are recalcitrant and no longer focused on the mission" and "do not measure up to their potential." (3) *Unsupportive faculty:* Another source of conflict surfaced when faculty did not support the direction of the department, for example, "chairs dealing with faculty resistance to improvements and change," "faculty acting unreasonably (and selfishly) and thereby causing turmoil and compromising the achievement of departmental objectives," and "when interpersonal differences between faculty inhibit the mission of the department and . . . basically work against the good of the department." (4) *Unsupportive chair:* Chairs also expressed remorse when they could not support their faculty and had "to make decisions which cause great disappointment to my colleagues" and "when I can't or don't have the resources to reward good faculty." (5) *Role of evaluation:* Although evaluation is inherent to their role, chairs reported difficulty in having to "evaluate their colleagues," "conduct annual reviews," "make tough decisions on merit evaluations and salaries," and "fire faculty." (6) *Role of mediation:* Finally, the chairs' failure to mediate conflict among their colleagues caused them to be dissatisfied. Generally, one chair expressed concern over "severe faculty confrontations" and another expressed difficulty "when I have to referee bad interpersonal relations between faculty" (Gmelch and Miskin, 1993, pp. 104–105).

All of these forces place department chairs in a role plagued with interpersonal conflict. In order to foresee and respond effectively to these crises and pressures, chairs need to be equipped with creative conflict management skills.

Positional Influence of Department Conflict

Department chairs are socialized as scholars first. Their socialization begins at graduate school and runs through the faculty ranks for approximately eighteen years before most faculty move into the chair position (Carroll, 1991). As faculty transform into chairs, they typically shift from a focus on scholarship activities to a focus on fragmented meetings and interruptions; from a feeling of autonomy to pursue one's own interests to a feeling that both faculty and administration controls one's time, activities, and actions; from professing in the classroom to persuading in meetings and political arenas; from a solitary work style to social collective action; from receiving department resources to allocating resources; and from writing manuscripts to writing memorandums (Gmelch and Miskin, 1995). A shift also occurs between the chair's personal life and professional life. Thus, two types of role conflict occur as faculty move into administration: the tension between balancing personal and professional lives and the conflict between the chair's academic and administrative roles.

Personal and Professional Role Conflict. As faculty move into administrative roles, have they been able to keep a balance between their administrative and personal lives? Or do they perceive they have accepted the leadership challenge at the expense of the personal pleasures? One of the costs to professors when they enter the chair position is the expenditure of time. Since time is inelastic and irreplaceable, chairs must try to balance their personal time with their newly acquired administrative responsibilities. In a study by the Center for the Study of the Department Chair (Gmelch, 1991), department chairs were asked whether they had spent more, the same, or less time in personal activities since they became chairs. What had occurred was a dramatic shift in time spent in professional activities at the cost of their personal lives: 65 percent of chairs reported spending less time with family, 56 percent with friends, and 77 percent with leisure activities due to administrative duties.

These same chairs were asked if they were satisfied with their shift in time allocations. Of those chairs who had sacrificed personal time for professional responsibilities, an overwhelming percentage expressed dissatisfaction with debiting their time with family (89 percent), friends (87.5 percent), and leisure activities (80.5 percent). Thus, a dramatic shift in personal and professional time occurs as faculty move into administration, resulting in tremendous dissatisfaction among the department chairs with this role conflict.

Academic Administration Role Conflict. Managers, who perform liaison or linkage roles in organizations, often find themselves in role conflict situations (Kahn and others, 1974). Academic department chairs encounter even greater role conflict since they are in a somewhat unique position without common management parallels. Department chairs seem to be trapped between the pressures and demands of performing not only as administrators but also as productive faculty members. Ambiguity and role conflict result from attempting to bridge the administrative and academic cores of the university, which are organized and operated differently (Bare, 1986). The academic core of teaching and research operates freely and independently in a loosely coupled system, whereas the managerial core maintains the mechanistic qualities of a tightly coupled system. The department chair is at the heart of the tension between the two systems. While this dynamic conflict between administration and academics is critical in order to maintain higher education organizations, it does place the department chair in the difficult position of mediating between the demands of administration and faculty. The chair feels trapped between the pressures to perform as a faculty member and as an administrator. These pressures, unique to department chairs, define their Janus-like position: Chairs are seen with both faculty member and administrator faces. This posture leads to split loyalties, mixed commitment, and heightened role conflict.

Creating a Healthy Web of Tension

No matter what the answer or reaction, one of the chair's main functions is to adjudicate these conflicting situations by creating a healthy web of tension. How should department chairs respond to conflict within their departments? My goal here in recognizing the nature of institutional conflict is not to debate whether the conflict from these organizational characteristics is negative or positive, controllable or uncontrollable, but rather to help prepare department chairs to respond appropriately when it arises. Chairs need to realize that regardless of the causes, it is their personal responsibility to respond to these conflict situations.

"Conflicts stem basically from differences among persons and groups. Elimination of conflict would mean the elimination of such differences. The goal of conflict management is, for us, better conceived as the acceptance and enhancement of differences among persons and groups" (Bennis, Benne, and Chen, 1969, p. 152). The strategy chairs should use, therefore, is to (1) manage the inevitable interpersonal conflict reflected in the second sphere of the web of conflict and (2) develop a personal approach to redesigning one's chair position to address the inherent role conflict between personal and professional pressures as well as the ambiguity of their competing academic and administrative roles.

Interpersonal Conflict: Principled Resolution. This chapter is not about how to win in a battle against faculty, but how to deal with differences such that all parties find a satisfying resolution, enjoy mutual respect, and maintain positive and productive relationships. The technique of *principled* resolution, as espoused by Fisher and Ury (1991), provides a straightforward approach to conflict. This method is especially appropriate in academic settings, where both outcome and relationships are simultaneously important. In contrast to positional or power resolution, the principled method focuses on (1) basic interests of both faculty and department chairs, (2) mutually satisfying options, and (3) fair standards and procedures, which, in combination, typically result in (4) wise outcomes or agreement.

The above four principles enable chairs to change the rules of the game and approach conflict from a principled point of view such that they approach faculty as mutual problem solvers, seeking a wise outcome by exploring and yielding to principle, not pressure. Once department chairs learn how to use this process, they will be able to deal with faculty empathetically as human beings, in search of a satisfying resolution and amicable agreement.

Personal and Professional Role Conflict: Principle-Centered Leadership. Two types of positional conflicts occur when faculty move into administrative roles. Chairs first need to learn how to balance their personal and professional demands and then make sure their professional pressures between the academic and administrative sides are productive and compatible. Some of the conflict problems of the chair position are structural and inherent to the way in which colleges and universities are organized; other conflict problems are personal and rooted in how chairs manage themselves.

The positional role conflict and ambiguity must be balanced and harmonized. Chairs need to take stock of their interests, values, and time in order to resolve this third and most introspective source of conflict. Covey, Merrill, and Merrill (1994) took a dramatically different approach to time and professional management—a principle-centered approach. It transcends the traditional prescriptions of working faster, harder, and smarter and offers not another clock but a compass because with conflict management it is more important where one is headed than how fast one is going.

In conclusion, this chapter illuminates some of the threads in the web of conflict in which department chairs find themselves entangled. It is not intended to repeat the concepts and practices involved in both principled conflict resolution and principle-centered time management. However, chairs are encouraged to search for their own principles to resolve their personal and professional conflicts. Also, the following books are suggested additions to chairs' professional libraries: *Getting to Yes: Negotiating Agreement Without Giving In* (Fisher and Ury, 1991), *Getting Past No: Negotiating with Difficult People* (Ury,

1991), and *First Things First* (Covey, Merrill, and Merrill, 1994). Let me repeat that "higher education will continue to have a 'leadership crisis' if the conditions for chairing a department remain an unmanageable and unproductive option for faculty. The answers to attracting and retaining effective departmental leaders may be in how the position is structured and how department chairs' time is utilized. We must create qualities that make the chair more attractive, tenable, and meaningful for promising professors" (Gmelch and Miskin, 1995, p. 138).

References

Baldridge, J. V. *Power and Conflict in the University.* New York: Wiley, 1971.

Bare, A. "Managerial Behavior of College Chairpersons and Administrators." *Research in Higher Education,* 1986, 24 (2), 128–138.

Birnbaum, R. *How Colleges Work: The Cybernetics of Academic Organization and Leadership.* San Francisco: Jossey-Bass, 1988.

Bennis, W. G., Benne, K. D., and Chen, R. *The Planning of Change.* (2nd ed.) Troy, Mo.: Holt, Rinehart & Winston, 1969.

Carroll, J. B. "Career Paths of Department Chairs." *Research in Higher Education,* 1991, 32 (6), 669–688.

Cohen, M. D., and March, J. G. *Leadership and Ambiguity: The American College President.* New York: McGraw-Hill, 1974.

Corwin, R. G. "Patterns of Organizational Conflict." *Administrative Science Quarterly,* 1969, 14, 507–520.

Covey, S. R., Merrill, A. R., and Merrill, R. R. *First Things First.* New York: Simon & Schuster, 1994.

Etzioni, A. *A Comparative Analysis of Complex Organizations: On Power, Involvement, and Their Correlates.* New York: Free Press, 1964.

Fisher, R., and Ury, W. *Getting to Yes: Negotiating Agreement Without Giving In.* New York: Penguin Books, 1991.

French, J.R.P., Jr., and Raven, B. "The Bases of Social Power." In D. Cartwright and A. Zander (eds.), *Group Dynamics: Research and Theory.* New York: HarperCollins, 1968.

Gmelch, W. H. "Paying the Price for Academic Leadership: Department Chair Tradeoffs." *Educational Record,* 1991, 72 (3), 45–49.

Gmelch, W. H., Carroll, J. B., Seedorf, R., and Wentz, D. *Center for the Study of the Department Chair: 1990 Survey.* Pullman: Washington State University, 1990.

Gmelch, W. H., and Miskin, V. D. *Leadership Skills for Department Chairs.* Bolton, Mass.: Anker, 1993.

Gmelch, W. H., and Miskin, V. D. *Chairing the Academic Department.* Thousand Oaks, Calif.: Sage, 1995.

Kahn, R. L., Wolfe, D. M., Quinn, R. P., Snoek, J. D., and Rosenthal, R. A. *Organizational Stress: Studies in Role Conflict and Ambiguity.* New York: Wiley, 1974.

Robbins, S. P. *Managing Organizational Conflict.* Englewood Cliffs, N.J.: Prentice Hall, 1974.

Simmel, G. *Conflict.* New York: Free Press, 1955.

Ury, W. *Getting Past No: Negotiating with Difficult People.* New York: Bantam Books, 1991.

Weick, K. E. "Educational Organizations as Loosely Coupled Systems." *Administrative Science Quarterly,* 1976, 21, 1–19.

WALTER H. GMELCH *is chair of and professor of educational administration in the Department of Educational Leadership and Counseling Psychology at Washington State University, Pullman, where he also serves as director of the Center for the Study of the Department Chair.*

Conflict between faculty and administrators is an age-old
problem. This chapter presents eight reasons for the difficult
relationship between these two subcultures of the academy.

Can't Live With Them,
Can't Live Without Them:
Faculty and Administrators in Conflict

Susan A Holton, Gerald Phillips

Since the dawn of academia, faculty and administrators have worked together and have disagreed. The current catch-phrase "you just don't understand," used to describe miscommunication between men and women (Tannen, 1990), could be applied to faculty and administrators because the occupants of these two worlds often do not understand each other. Faculty bemoan the lack of support by administrators, administrators wonder what faculty actually do. The two often lack sufficient appreciation for the importance of each other's jobs and often view each other as "opposing camps" on campus.

Faculty often react strongly against administrators. "In many places, it manifests itself in genteel teasing and friendly scorn for the seemingly unintellectual, and therefore undemanding nature of the administrator's job. In other places, it takes on uglier tones, leading to a Pavlovian, knee-jerk aversion and contempt for all things administrative in character, culminating in some individuals in a permanent state of ill-concealed disrespect for all ranks above full professor" (Morris, 1981, p. 18). Administrators often see faculty as "highly verbal and inquisitive, resplendent of ego and hubris and blessed with a well-developed sense of both their own social importance and special rights as intellectuals in an essentially Philistine social order" (Morris, 1981, p. 6).

Eight Reasons for Faculty-Administrator Conflict

As one who served in multiple capacities on the faculty side of the aisle, Gerald Phillips possessed unique insight into the academic world. His eight reasons that faculty and administrators engage in conflict form the basis of this chapter.

REASON 1: Being an administrator is not a promotion for a professor, it is a new career path.

For years, administrators, especially academic administrators and presidents, have come from the faculty. The assumption is that just because one is a good professor, he or she will be a good chair, and then administrator. "These beliefs persist in faculty folk wisdom even through most people who have occupied any of these positions for even a brief time recognize the limitations of this way of thinking" (Ehrle and Bennett, 1988, p. vii).

Because of this system of advancing from the ranks of the faculty, administrators are often not prepared for their job. And while leadership institutes for faculty and administrators are now being established on campuses throughout the country, they are a relatively new phenomenon. Two notable, long-standing programs are Higher Education Resource Services Institute for Women in Higher Education Administration, which was founded twenty-five years ago, and Harvard Institute for Educational Management (see McDade and Lewis, 1994).

Not only is the move from faculty to administrator a different career path, it is often seen as "going over to the enemy" and entering the "other world." While there is an overall campus culture, there are distinct worlds or subcultures of faculty and administrators. The subcultures are seen as "distinct, even alien in . . . [their] commitments, priorities, values, and assumptions" (Kuhn and Whitt, 1988, p. 92).

These differences constitute one of the reasons for faculty-administrator conflict. Eugene Rice, former faculty member and administrator and now director of the Forum on Faculty Roles and Rewards at the American Association of Higher Education (AAHE) notes, "One cause of conflict in higher education is that administrators are no longer out of the faculty; they don't share the same culture" (personal communication, March 23, 1995). Thomas Angelo, a college teacher and administrator who currently directs the AAHE's Assessment Forum, notes that "conflict is more prevalent now. Over time, there has been greater distance between who administrators and faculty are. In the past, administrators came up through the ranks of faculty. Now they often come from elsewhere, or didn't spend much time as faculty. So not much is shared, and administrators don't understand why faculty are the way they are" (personal communication, March 20, 1995).

These cultural differences are especially obvious in the conflict between faculty and student affairs administrators. These two groups of people see education in vastly different ways. Student affairs professionals see their work as educational, and professors do not always agree with this assessment (Blimling, 1982).

REASON 2: Professors and administrators answer to different authorities.

Who is the authority for the campus community? For faculty and administrators, the answers are different. Faculty members identify far more with their disciplines than with their institutions. "Culture of the discipline is the primary source of faculty identity and expertise and typically engenders stronger bonds than those developed within the institution of employment, particularly in large universities" (Kuhn and Whitt, 1988, p. 77).

Because they have different authorities, faculty and administrators have different role expectations as well. Both believe in academic freedom. But the perceived ramifications of academic freedom may be different for the two groups. In research on academic freedom, Ambrose (1989, pp. 91–92) found that "significant differences exist between what the respondents felt about the concept and how they would apply academic freedom to specific circumstances on campus. . . . The differences among faculty members, department chairs, and administrators concerning the range or scope of academic freedom within specific circumstances may be attributed more to role behavior or role responsibilities than to the affects of an academic or administrative culture within their colleges."

REASON 3: *Policy is always in conflict with local option. The independence of the tenured full professor is often an affront to the administrator.*

Green (1990, p. 6) addressed this point when she noted that "the old quip that faculty members want leadership until they get it has more than a grain of truth to it. Indeed, colleges and universities are inherently resistant to leadership."

Working with faculty is seen, by many administrators, as a difficult task. The phrase "working with faculty is like herding cats" certainly reflects the independence of the faculty member, and the difficulty that the administrator may have because of that independence: "In the faculty's subconscious also lurks the notion that the work they do, teaching and research, is a kind of activity that does not require towering structures of organizational apparatus to make it work. . . . In the faculty's view, a university is a kind of place that can more or less run itself once the faculty and students are brought in touch with one another. Administrators, they believe, are superfluous, make-work bureaucrats who interfere with the main business of the institution and who, with their huge salaries, divert resources from what a university is all about" (Morris, 1981, p. 19).

Administrators have to carry out the policy established by groups who are often not on campus—legislatures, boards of regents, and other governing bodies. Their policies are not always agreed upon by faculty, who may be reluctant, or who are seen as recalcitrant, in adhering to those policies.

REASON 4: *There are persistent irritations—personality conflict, jealousy, tenure and promotion decisions, hiring decisions, new courses, course assignments, policy, and, of course, parking.*

Whenever two people gather, interpersonal conflict is possible; if there are perceived inequities, conflict is probable. On college campuses, there are perceived inequities in freedom, in salary, in "perks," and more. These conflicts are, of course, exacerbated by the nature of the decisions and decision-making process of faculty and administrators.

In many institutions, the administrators work in what may be perceived as lavish settings with adequate support staff and money for travel and professional memberships—especially from the perspective of faculty, who are confined to windowless, obscure offices with little or no secretarial support and often minuscule budgets. "Being an administrator carries the trappings of luxury . . . the office, secretarial and administrative assistance, the use of the car, a better travel budget, and so forth" (Spees, 1989, p. 20). And being an administrator may give the all-coveted perk—a parking place—while faculty scramble for a spot.

Another differential causing conflict is salaries. Eugene Rice (personal communication, March 23, 1995) notes that "in the 80s there developed a great salary differential between faculty and administrators. So both of these, salary and culture, must be addressed." This differential continues today.

A factor in these conflicts is the perceived concern for the institution. While many faculty members feel that they will be members of the institution for life, they think that administrators will not be. Based on his research on faculty, Robert Diamond, assistant vice chancellor at Syracuse University, concludes that "faculty often perceive administrators as transients. They, the faculty, believe that they'll be around longer and administrators will go away. There is a high turnover in administration" (personal communication, March 20, 1995). Thus, faculty perceive that decisions made by an administrator are likely to be overturned—by the next administrator. If the faculty member merely waits long enough, and stalls long enough, the administrator may be gone.

REASON 5: *Standards of judgment are never clear. Professors do not really understand how they are judged on teaching, service, and scholarship. The roles of student evaluation, peer evaluation, and evaluation by the higher-ups are not always clear.*

How *are* faculty judged? In many institutions, the answer is not clear. Anecdotes abound of faculty who published and yet perished because of what they perceived as an administrative whim. In many institutions, lip service is given to the equality of teaching, service, and scholarship, until tenure time when teaching and service are overshadowed by research and published scholarship.

In addition, faculty often feel that they do not need to be monitored, supervised, or interfered with by administrators. According to Morris (1981, p. 19), faculty members often view themselves as above the fray, as people who are more intelligent than the average citizen and, therefore, not in need of supervision: "This benign self-concept among university professors probably stems from a halo effect surrounding the intelligentsia in every society, namely, that since they are demonstrably more intelligent and articulate than their fellow citizens, they must also be better as people, i.e., more sensitive, responsive, cooperative, and generous. Working from this nonsequitur, faculty members find the surveillance of superiors uncomfortable, an insult to their sense of rectitude and motivational purity, and an institutionalized questioning of their niceness."

REASON 6: *Professors are urgent for input. That means they want their own way. Administrators want to give the illusion of input. That means they will have their own way and act like it was democratically decided.*

How are decisions made in academia? What role do faculty have—or administrators? In some institutions, the theory of decision making is clearly delineated but the practice may still be a conundrum.

A part of the problem is the lack of vision and mission—and acknowledgment of reality—in many institutions. Thomas Angelo (personal communication, March 20, 1995) notes that "there are very unrealistic expectations by departments, and by some institutions, trying to create something they're not. It creates dysfunctional conflict. For example, you go to a state university and people want to publish and get grants. Pushing that causes conflict and keeps faculty from doing what they should do. There is pressure to do things that are not consistent with the institution's reality. There are not enough lifeboats on the Titanic." Robert Diamond (personal communication, March 20, 1995) concurs. "A major disagreement exists between where administrators are pushing institutions, and where faculty want it to go. Faculty perceive administrators as setting themselves up for their next job. Faculty feel that administrators give only 'lip service' to the importance of teaching."

Institutions across the continent are engaged in significant change as the reality of the 1990s requires downsizing and different answers to the problems plaguing academia. And, too often, administrators and faculty are not equally involved in the decision making, which leads to conflict. According to Diamond (personal communication, March 20, 1995), "In significant change, administrators aren't involving faculty, aren't getting them into the political change process. In order to go about institutional change, you must have ownership, have the administrators get faculty involved. Faculty say administrators will change, so why bother? Administrators often feel that faculty are pains in the butt."

In some institutions, there is a sense that faculty do not care or are not paying attention to the institutions, that they are focused only on their own classroom experience. According to higher education researcher Robert Blackburn (personal communication, April 26, 1995), "There is a great tension between administration and faculty. More faculty aren't paying much attention to what happens in central administration."

But decision making is never easy. How much should everyone be involved in the decision making? "A contemporary academic administrator walks daily through mine fields of irony. A faculty that considers itself slighted if virtually any decision is made without its having been consulted, nevertheless expects its president singlehandedly to transform any opponent's value system" (Plante, 1988, p. 77).

REASON 7: *It is rarely clear to either party how much power each has and how each can affect the other. The professor is a potential saboteur or guerrilla. The administrator is an obstacle.*

Who is really in charge in the academy? The answer is not always clear and thus a cause of conflict at many institutions. Part of that confusion is owing to the nature of higher education, which Weick (1976) referred to as "loosely coupled systems." He noted that while faculty and administrators (and other groups) are united, each also stays a separate entity: "Two units or people may be somehow attached, but each retains some identity and separateness; their attachment may be circumscribed, infrequent, weak in its mutual affects, unimportant, and/or slow to respond. Loose coupling also carries connotations of impermanence, dissolvability, and tacitness, all of which are potentially crucial properties of the 'glue' that holds organizations together" (Weick, 1976, p. 544).

The relationship between faculty and administrators is reflected in many of the ways in which conflict can be created in their work. The levels of hierarchy, rules and regulations, nature of supervision, participation in decision making, sources of power, rewards and recognition, staff interdependence, and roles and responsibilities all contribute to potential conflict within the academy (Gmelch and Carroll, 1991).

There is always a question of who is in charge in academia. Where is the true leadership? Green (1990, p. 6) posed this question as follows: "If faculty members are the heart of an institution, what real 'leadership' role can administrators have? The ability of faculty members to exercise leadership among peers is also limited by the academic culture. Academicians regard the overt exercise of power with suspicion and distaste."

While there are questions of power and who holds power in academia, it is also clear that power can be transforming. If power is seen as "power to" rather than "power over," then the exercise of that power can contribute positively to the institution.

Institutional leadership can and does make a difference in institutional morale. "Indeed, we have found that in the ten high-morale colleges visited, the institutional leaders were critical forces in maintaining distinctive organizational cultures and enhancing faculty morale. . . . This study also has shown that high levels of work satisfaction and morale among faculty are related to a sense of joint ownership of the college. This sense of commonly shared mission and ownership is fostered by the institutional leadership" (Council of Independent Colleges, 1987).

REASON 8: *There are natural irritations in any boss-employee relationship and despite protestations to the contrary, the administrator is a boss.*

Organizational development research abounds noting tensions between boss and employee. That situation also characterizes the world of the academic organization.

But some say that faculty act as if they have no bosses. Blackburn, Horowitz, Edington, and Klos (1986, p. 37) found that "one might conclude either that faculty do not perceive that they have supervisors or else that their supervisors do not serve as a source of job stress. . . . For administrators, there is a significant association between job strain and their satisfaction with their supervisor. . . . For faculty, work is life, and a low estimation of the professorial life is translated into a low quality of life as well." With this attitude, it is obviously difficult when any administrator attempts to exert authority in working with faculty.

This boss-employee relationship frequently leads to a breakdown of friendship between faculty and administrators. Morris (1981, p. 22) suggested that once one becomes an administrator, he or she must give up personal ties to faculty, that the mix of power and subordination are "inimical to the act of friendship."

Natural Affiliation of Faculty and Administrators

Even with interpersonal and role conflict, faculty and administrators are still integral parts of the same system; both are necessary in the orderly functioning of the academic institutions. Eble (1978, p. 2) discussed the dangers of separation of faculty and administrators:

> Regarding administration as too new a country also has adverse effects. It increases the seeming separation of the academic from the administrative when they are actually and necessarily intertwined. It magnifies the distances between an administrator and former faculty colleagues which increase over time and as one rises in the administrative ranks. It can result in faculty and administration occupying separate territories, each jealous of its rights and seldom hospitable even to friendly visits. All of these are reasons for urging faculty members who enter administration to do so in a more roguish spirit, to start out with a spirit of adventure, and to keep in touch with the folks back home.

References

Ambrose, C. M. "A Comparison of Faculty Members' and Administrators' Definitions of and Attitudes Toward Academic Freedom." Unpublished doctoral dissertation, Department of Educational Administration, University of Georgia, 1989.

Blackburn, R., Horowitz, S. M., Edington, D. W., and Klos, D. M. "University Faculty and Administrator Responses to Job Strains." *Research in Higher Education*, 1986, 25 (1), 31–41.

Blimling, G. S. "The Context of Conflict in the Academy: An Educational Dialectic on Faculty and Student Affairs Educators." *College Student Affairs Journal*, 1982, *13* (1), 4–12.

Boyer, E. L. *College: The Undergraduate Experience in America.* New York: HarperCollins, 1987.

Council of Independent Colleges. *Community, Commitment, and Congruence: A Different Kind of Excellence.* Washington, D.C.: Council of Independent Colleges, 1987.

Eble, K. E. *The Art of Administration: A Guide for Academic Administrators.* San Francisco: Jossey-Bass, 1978.

Ehrle, E. B., and Bennett, J. B. *Managing the Academic Enterprise: Case Studies for Deans and Provosts.* New York: American Council on Education/Macmillan, 1988.

Gmelch, W. H., and Carroll, J. B. "The 3Rs of Conflict Management for Department Chairs and Faculty." *Innovative Higher Education*, 1991, *16* (2), 107–123.

Green, M. "Investing in Leadership." *Liberal Education*, 1990, *76* (1), 6–13.

Kuhn, G. D., and Whitt, E. J. *The Invisible Tapestry: Culture in American Colleges and Universities.* ASHE-ERIC Higher Education Report No. 1. Washington, D.C.: Association for the Study of Higher Education, 1988.

McDade, S. A., and Lewis, P. H. (eds.). *Developing Administrative Excellence: Creating a Culture of Leadership.* New Directions for Higher Education, no. 87. San Francisco: Jossey-Bass, 1994.

Morris, V. C. *Deaning: Middle Management in Academe.* Urbana: University of Illinois Press, 1981.

Plante, P. R., and Caret, R. I. *Myths and Realities of Academic Administration.* New York: American Council on Education/Macmillan, 1988.

Spees, E. R. *Higher Education: An Arena of Conflicting Philosophies.* New York: Lang, 1989.

Tannen, D. *You Just Don't Understand: Women and Men in Conversation.* New York: William Morrow, 1990.

Weick, K. E. "Educational Organizations as Loosely Coupled Systems." *Administrative Science Quarterly*, 1976, *21*, 1–19.

SUSAN A HOLTON *is professor of communication studies at Bridgewater State College, Bridgewater, Massachusetts, and director of the Massachusetts Faculty Development Consortium.*

GERALD PHILLIPS, *now deceased, was professor emeritus at Pennsylvania State University, University Park.*

This chapter explores the extent and scope of academic collective bargaining as a model for conflict resolution.

From Conflict to Accord: Collective Bargaining at the Academy

Frank R. Annunziato

The labor and management advocates of collective bargaining have argued over the years that the processes leading to the enactment (negotiations) and enforcement (grievance and arbitration procedures) of collective bargaining agreements provide a powerful model to identify and resolve conflicts that arise between employers and employees. The great advantage of collective bargaining over other methods of conflict resolution is that individual disputes are channeled to agents for each side. The union, by law, is the collective bargaining agent for all employees (members of the bargaining unit). For employers, the firm designates specific officials within its hierarchy to act on its behalf. Together, relatively small groups discuss and, it is hoped, resolve conflicts affecting many more people on both sides.

There are two objectives to this chapter. First, I explore the extent to which collective bargaining, as a model for conflict resolution, has permeated the nation's colleges and universities. Second, I present and analyze extracts from several faculty collective bargaining agreements to emphasize the unique nature of collective bargaining as a model for conflict resolution. All information in this chapter on faculty collective bargaining in higher education is taken from *Directory of Faculty Contracts and Bargaining Agents in Institutions of Higher Education* (Annunziato, 1995).

Since 1969, the year of the first faculty-university collective bargaining agreement in the United States between the City University of New York (CUNY) and the Professional Staff Congress (PSC), the collective bargaining model of conflict resolution has found fertile ground at the nation's colleges and universities, although the extent of its development is limited almost exclusively to public sector institutions and by geography. In 1995, academic unions represented 242,221 faculty members in 502 bargaining units on 1,075 campuses. Four-year institutions can account for 138,254 of the total number of unionized professors; another 103,967 teach at two-year colleges. While the process of collective bargaining has declined throughout the United States economy to less than 16 percent of all eligible workers in 1994, faculty collective bargaining, with approximately 25 to 30 percent of the professoriat represented by unions, is one of the most highly unionized occupations in the country. In 1994 alone, faculty unions won eight out of eleven collective bargaining elections, involving almost 2,000 professors.

A Public Sector Phenomenon

Although union density among college and university faculty is substantially higher than in the general working population, the overwhelming number of faculty members covered by collective bargaining agreements teach at public colleges and universities, at the state, municipal, and county levels. During 1994, public sector institutions employed 231,496 faculty members, or 95.5 percent of the total number of unionized professors, with 432 bargaining units on 987 campuses.

Among public institutions, there is an almost even division between four-year and two-year schools. Four-year public institutions employ 128,116 faculty members, or 55 percent of all unionized faculty at all public institutions (128,116/231,496). Two-year public schools employ 103,380 unionized professors, or 45 percent of all unionized faculty at all public institutions (103,380/231,496).

There are only 10,725 unionized faculty members in the nation's private colleges and universities, with 70 bargaining units on 88 campuses. The vast majority of these are employed at private four-year colleges and universities: 10,138 professors, with 60 bargaining units on 74 campuses. Unions only represent 587 faculty members on 14 two-year private sector campuses, in 10 bargaining units.

One can attribute the small number of unionized private colleges and universities primarily to an extremely unfavorable legal environment. The United States Supreme Court in 1980, by a narrow five to four majority, issued its *Yeshiva* decision, which determined that under certain circumstances faculty members at private colleges and universities are managers and, therefore, not employees as defined by the National Labor Relations Act. The majority opinion in *Yeshiva* stated,

> The controlling consideration in this case is that the faculty of Yeshiva University exercise authority which in any other context unquestionably would be managerial. Their authority in academic matters is absolute. They decide what courses will be offered, when they will be scheduled, and to whom they will be taught. They debate and determine teaching methods, grading policies, and

matriculation standards. They effectively decide which students will be admitted, retained and graduated. . . . When one considers the function of a university, it is difficult to imagine decisions more managerial than these [*National Labor Relations Board v. Yeshiva University*, 444 U.S. 672, 103 LRRM 2526 (1980)].

The Court's decision did not automatically eliminate faculty collective bargaining rights at all private colleges and universities. In effect, the Court ordered the National Labor Relations Board (NLRB) to apply the indicia for managerial authority established in *Yeshiva* to all other private colleges and universities. As a result, a number of private colleges that had established faculty collective bargaining units prior to *Yeshiva* successfully asked NLRB to decertify, or eliminate, their faculty unions. For example, NLRB decertified faculty unions at Ashland College (Ohio), Boston University (Massachusetts), Catholic University Law School (Washington, D.C.), College of Osteopathic Medicine (Iowa), Fairleigh Dickinson University (New Jersey), University of Dubuque (Iowa), University of New Haven (Connecticut), University of Pittsburgh (Pennsylvania), Wagner College (New York), and at least 20 other private colleges.

After *Yeshiva*, faculty unions found it increasingly more difficult to organize new unions. By 1995, only 70 private sector colleges and university collective bargaining agents existed, representing fewer than 5 percent of all unionized professors. Some of these private institutions with collective bargaining voluntarily continued a relationship with their faculty unions after *Yeshiva*, such as at the University of San Francisco (California), Regis University (Colorado), Mitchell College (Connecticut), and Emerson College (Massachusetts).

NLRB did not find that faculty members at all schools possess the same degree of managerial authority that *Yeshiva* required. In such schools as Wentworth Institute (Massachusetts), Kendall School of Design (Michigan), Pratt Institute (New York), and Stevens Institute of Technology (New Jersey), NLRB ruled that their faculty members were nonmanagerial employees and therefore protected by federal labor relations law. NLRB allowed collective bargaining status for faculty members at these institutions.

State-by-State Distribution

Since the National Labor Relations Act is only applicable to the private sector economy, public sector faculty unions are not restricted by the mandates of the *Yeshiva* decision. Public sector collective bargaining operates under labor relations law established at the state level. While faculty collective bargaining agents exist in thirty-three states, Washington, D.C., and Guam, faculty higher education collective bargaining is geographically limited. Two states, California (66,076) and New York (55,250), account for 121,326, or 50 percent, of all unionized faculty members. The ten largest states (see Table 7.1) for faculty collective bargaining represent 201,295, or 83 percent, of the unionized professoriat. Five of these largest states are located in the northeast (New York, Pennsylvania, New Jersey, Connecticut, and Massachusetts) and are the home states for 96,849 unionized professors, 40 percent of the total number. The two West Coast states, California (66,076) and Washington (9,189), represent another 75,265 faculty members, 31 percent of all unionized faculty. Stated another way, seven states, five in the northeast and two on the West Coast, account for 71 percent of unionized professors. Table 7.1 shows only two states in the Midwest, Michigan (10,307) and Illinois (7,985). Florida (10,899) is the only southern state to make this list.

The Unions

Faculty members desirous of collective bargaining have overwhelmingly opted for one of three national unions: American Association of University Professors (AAUP), American Federation of Teachers (AFT), and National Education Association (NEA). The largest of these three in terms of higher education membership, AFT, represents 84,706 professors. NEA is next with 69,338. AAUP is the collective bargaining agent for 18,632. However, these numbers do not include faculty members in merged organizations, or faculty bargaining agents who are affiliated with more than one national union. Table 7.2 shows those institutions that have merged unions. The inclusion of faculty members from merged organizations into the aggregate totals for the three largest national higher education unions significantly increases their sizes. AFT, including all its merged organizations, represents 102,917 faculty. NEA and its merged organizations is the bargaining agent for 88,365 professors. AAUP, and its merged organizations, represents 64,298 faculty members.

Table 7.1. Ten Largest States with Unionized Faculty

State	Number of Unionized Faculty
California	66,076
New York	55,250
Pennsylvania	11,491
Florida	10,889
New Jersey	10,610
Michigan	10,307
Connecticut	9,884
Massachusetts	9,614
Washington	9,189
Illinois	7,985

Another 19,552 professors have won collective bargaining rights through independent unions, which are organizations without state or national affiliations to other unions. Finally, 4,620 professors have chosen collective bargaining under the aegis of the American Federation of Government Employees, the American Federation of State, County, and Municipal Employees, the Communications Workers of America, the Service Employees International Union, and the United Auto Workers.

Conflict Resolution Broadly Defined

A cursory review of several faculty collective bargaining agreements discloses the breadth of topics that labor and management practitioners have now resolved through negotiations. Practitioners have brought academic as well as economic disputes to the bargaining table, involving professors, administrators,

Table 7.2. Institutions with Merged Unions

Institution	State	Bargaining Agents	Degree Period	Unit Size
California State University	California	AAUP/NEA	four year	18,400
Connecticut Community and Technical Colleges (administration only)	Connecticut	AFSCME/ CCCC	two year	725
Connecticut Community and Technical Colleges (community college faculty only)	Connecticut	CCCC/SEIU	two year	2,251
Belleville Area College	Illinois	AAUP/AFT	two year	125
City University of New York	New York	AAUP/AFT	four year	17,459
Saint John's University	New York	AAUP/IND	four year	920
Green River Community College	Washington	AFT/NEA	two year	223
Eastern Washington University	Washington	AFT/NEA	four year	404

Note: AAUP = American Association of University Professors; AFSCME = American Federation of State, County, and Municipal Employees; AFT = American Federation of Teachers; CCCC = Connecticut Congress of Community Colleges; IND = independent; NEA = National Education Association; SEIU = Service Employees International Union.

and even students. Since the *Yeshiva* decision's indicia of managerial authority do not apply to public colleges and universities, faculty unionists and administrators have bargained over issues and conflicts that cut to the heart of institutional academic mission.

The current contract (1990–1996) between CUNY and PSC, with more than ninety pages, prescribes economic and academic conflict resolution. While the CUNY-PSC contract establishes faculty salaries and fringe benefits, it also addresses traditional academic concerns such as appointments and reappointments, course workload, discipline of faculty, research fellowships, and faculty development.

On page 9 of the 1991–1994 contract between the Board of Regents of the State University System of Florida and the United Faculty of Florida, labor and management have negotiated the following interesting language on sexual harassment, which includes faculty, administrators, and students: "In addition to the parties' concern with respect to sexual harassment in the employment context, the parties also recognize the potential for this form of illegal discrimination against students. Relationships between employees and students, even if consensual, may become exploitative, and especially so when a student's academic work, residential life, or athletic endeavors are supervised or evaluated by the employee."

A private sector example of the breadth of issues tackled by academic unionists and administrators comes from the 1989–1990 contract between the small and elite Bard College and AAUP. Even granted the problems of managerial decision making prescribed by the *Yeshiva* decision, the language on pages 6–7 expresses the collective commitment of Bard's administration and its faculty union to the professors' academic wisdom and authority: "Subject, content and conduct, and size and criteria for admissions of courses are the responsibility of each teacher, subject to the direction and approval of his or her Departmental and Divisional Colleagues, and the regular elected Committees of the Faculty, and subject to review by Faculty meetings. The faculty has autonomy in academic affairs; e.g., the student-faculty ratio is an academic policy subject to faculty approval."

In addition, higher education collective bargaining agreements contain grievance and arbitration procedures to resolve conflicts arising during the terms of a contract, without resort to strikes, lockouts, or costly and lengthy judicial litigation. For example, the 1987–1991 agreement between the Board of Trustees of the California State University and the California Faculty Association allows a faculty member to bring a "faculty status matter," defined as "a dispute involving solely a decision not to reappoint, promote, or tenure," either to a peer review panel consisting of full-time tenured employees or to an independent and outside arbitrator for resolution.

One could have pointed out examples from hundreds of other contracts to prove the point: When a mutually respectful relationship exists between faculty unionists and administrators, only a lack of boldness and imagination can limit the scope of collective bargaining as a model for conflict resolution.

Reference

Annunziato, F. R. (ed.). *Directory of Faculty Contracts and Bargaining Agents in Institutions of Higher Education.* New York: National Center for the Study of Collective Bargaining in Higher Education and the Professions, School of Public Affairs, Baruch College, City University of New York, 1995.

FRANK R. ANNUNZIATO is director of the National Center for the Study of Collective Bargaining in Higher Education and the Professions, School of Public Affairs, Baruch College, City University of New York.

Universities as political systems function somewhere between
autocracy and anarchy—a fertile ground for institutional conflict.

Institutional Conflict

Allan W. Ostar

In the real world, which, by definition, lies outside the assumed but nonexistent walls of academe, conflict often arises between employers and employees, haves and have-nots, the enchanted and disenchanted, liberals and conservatives, and those who are part of the establishment versus those who are not. But in academe the roots of conflict are much more complex—everyone has ownership, and only grudgingly is one willing to acknowledge ownership by anyone else.

The faculty base their claim of ownership on often-repeated statements that a university is a community of scholars. Their claim is reinforced through faculty senates and general acceptance of the concept of shared governance.

The students say they have ownership because the university would not exist without them. Disillusioned students would like to turn the clock back to medieval times when the students hired and fired the faculty. In addition, students in both public and private institutions believe that since they are being required to pay ever-increasing shares of operating budgets through higher tuition and fees, they should have a voice in determining how those increases are allocated. Indeed, it is not uncommon to have one or more students on governing boards.

Feelings of ownership by loyal alumni are nurtured by encouragement of their continued involvement in university affairs. It is not surprising that this approach also helps enhance fundraising.

The governing boards in most cases have legal ownership, which they exercise through control of the budget, policy-making, and the hiring and firing of presidents. They establish the parameters for shared governance but believe that what they giveth, they can taketh away. At the same time they recognize that they are better off with shared governance than with shared ownership.

In the case of public institutions, the taxpayers claim ownership through their elected representatives, while in private institutions religious bodies, major donors, and others who provide significant financial or other support believe they have legitimate rights of ownership. They, too, believe that what they give they can take away, especially if the institutions they help fund are doing things they do not like, or are not doing things that they want them to do. If these feelings are strong enough, they may try to override or even change the membership of the governing board—actions that increasingly are a major source of conflict.

Nowhere are these multiple claims of ownership manifested more than in the process that higher education institutions follow in searching, screening, and selecting presidents and chancellors. Corporate executives express amazement that university search committees involve all the claimants of ownership in the process—faculty, students, alumni, midlevel administrators, support staff, board members, and even influential members of the communities in which the institutions are located. And they are even more amazed that the process generally takes five or six months.

In the corporate world, boards of directors hire professional "head-hunters," whose job it is to find the best-qualified person available. They can do so in a fraction of the time it takes a university because they do not have to be bothered with involving the employees, the stockholders, or the customers in the process.

The potential for institutional conflict is enormous in searches for university presidents and senior officials. At the outset of the search process each element of the greater university community has its own perception of the qualifications and experience desired in the person who is to be selected. And each element often will list a different set of institutional needs and priorities to be addressed. Faculty representatives, for example, want a president with a solid record of scholarly accomplishment who will command the respect of his or her colleagues and add academic luster to the institution, raise standards, and maintain the status quo. Board members, on the other hand, want someone with strong management experience who can deal with shrinking budgets, respond to calls for reform and change, do more and better with less, raise funds, increase enrollments, and skillfully practice public relations.

The real test of the chair of a search committee, increasingly aided by an outside search consultant, is the ability to get representatives of the various constituencies on the committee to reach consensus on institutional priorities. Only then can the representatives rise above their parochial interests and focus attention as a group on qualifications needed to address those priorities.

Obviously, the person finally selected will have a broader base of support and a much better chance of success when constituency conflicts are resolved early in the process. But if this is the case as the collegial process of searches becomes more widespread, why is it that the length of time presidents remain in office continues to get shorter? A pithy answer was offered at a meeting of presidents of state colleges and universities: "Friends come and go while enemies accumulate." Put another way, the growing intensity of institutional conflict is fraying time-honored principles of collegiality and civility as applied to relationships between and among the various components of the university community. Votes of no-confidence in the president are becoming more prevalent.

Peruse any issue of the *Chronicle of Higher Education* for examples of institutional conflict. Space devoted to news stories, opinion pieces, and letters to the editor related to institutional conflict is exceeded only by display advertising for positions available. There may even be some correlation between the two.

Conflicts du jour on any given issue may include affirmative action, political correctness, intercollegiate athletics, accreditation (read: accountability), race relations, perquisites for administrators, multiculturalism, tenure, research versus undergraduate teaching, treatment of laboratory animals, tuition policies, faculty workload, and productivity. Each of these issues can escalate quickly from reasoned discourse, as befits an academic institution, to adversarial and divisive positions. Under such circumstances, there is little hope for developing a sense of community. Community requires trust and a willingness to subordinate parochial interests in favor of the common good. Conflict is the enemy of community.

Conflict also makes news, so it is little wonder that public confidence is shaken in the ability of higher education to resolve its own problems. In consequence, public and private sponsors of higher education become more intrusive through calls for increased regulation, establishment of state and foundation commissions to review higher education policies, and threats to withhold support.

Pressure is put on governing boards to play a more active role in dealing with issues that result in conflict. The boards in turn put pressure on the presidents to take charge, bring about change, or get out. When the problems are exacerbated by budget cuts and the need to reduce programs and services with termination of tenured faculty, again it is not surprising that presidents are not remaining in office as long as they used to.

Pick any two or three recent issues of the *Chronicle of Higher Education* at random for items that reflect institutional conflict: The president of Rosemont College resigns when the board of trustees asks her to cancel a campus art exhibit about undergarments. Students at Rutgers University clash with police during a sit-in as part of an effort to force the president to resign over his remark, for which he apologized, that African Americans lack the "genetic hereditary background" to do well on admissions tests. Students at Northwestern University go on a hunger strike to demand establishment of an Asian studies department. Battle lines are drawn on affirmative action on many college campuses. Many of the most vocal critics of political correctness want to impose their own version (opinion). Entrenched segregation at most Southern universities is disenfranchising new generations of minority students (new study). The person who is hired to manage the president's house at the University of Pennsylvania will not have to walk the president's dog or tutor her kids after all. Faculty leaders at Boston University are so angry about the way their next president was selected that they hold a referendum to condemn the process. Wellesley is about to learn if it is possible to have a civilized debate about the soundness of its multicultural requirement. Three professors sue the University of Iowa claiming that its elimination of the Department of Dental Hygiene amounts to sex discrimination because all of the students and professors in the program are women. Campus police at the University of New Mexico give special treatment to two basketball players who admitted to a burglary. A U.S. district court rules that Brown University discriminates against its female athletes. A federal judge orders Alabama's two public, historically black universities to become less black, infuriating lawyers for black citizens. A judge rules that the University of Minnesota must make public some records of its use of animals in research. Dozens of students at DePaul University occupy the offices of the student newspaper in protest of what they claim is racism at the university.

Institutional conflict is not a new phenomenon. One way universities have served society since the Middle Ages is by providing an environment that encourages freedom to search for truth, to explore new ideas no matter how outrageous or unpopular, and to allow faculty and students to think otherwise without fear of retribution. Properly employed, conflict can be the catalyst for advancing wisdom with the goal of improving the human condition.

But conflict becomes destructive when it is used as an instrument for power politics. It undermines the concept of the university as community. When Robben Fleming was president of the University of Michigan during a period when institutional conflict was intensifying, he said, "If the university community, both faculty and students, is unwilling to face the responsibility which internal discipline requires, it is clear that the public will insist that order be imposed from the outside." Universities are very much at risk when rational discourse is replaced by conflict as the means for resolving campus issues.

ALLAN W. OSTAR is adjunct professor of higher education at Pennsylvania State University, University Park. He served for twenty-six years as president of the American Association of State Colleges and Universities until his retirement in 1991, when he became a senior consultant with the Academic Search Consultation Service.

Universities are immersed in various forms of conflict as they go about the business of education, but none is more perplexing than the town-and-gown conflict encountered with host communities.

Town and Gown: Forums for Conflict and Consensus Between Universities and Communities

Wallace Warfield

A university's relationship with the surrounding community is often marked by a certain ambivalence. The notion of an ivory tower, a bastion of intellect and learning, can bring prestige and a certain cache to the community in which it resides. Residents will comment with pride to visitors that sons and daughters have gone to the nearby university, that an institution of higher learning in a given community has produced a Nobel Prize winner or features an outstanding athletic team and so on. This relationship is enhanced by the fact that most institutions of higher education have opened their doors to local citizens and organizations through the extension of university services in training, research, and other endeavors. For example, adult education programs are a popular form of outreach to host communities. At George Mason University's Institute for Conflict Analysis and Resolution, a practicum has recently been established that places teams of students in surrounding communities to work with officials, local leadership, and residents in designing responses to various forms of conflict.

From an economic standpoint, colleges and universities can be important sources of income, sustaining local businesses. As well, private institutions generate dependable tax revenue streams for local governments.

But a university's relationship with its host community is not all sweetness and light. Relationships are frequently marred by a multitude of conflictual interactions, including student housing off campus, traffic congestion, and complaints from local residents about student behavior, to name a few. In

NEW DIRECTIONS FOR HIGHER EDUCATION, no. 92, Winter 1995 © Jossey-Bass Publishers

smaller communities, where economic and class differences separate middle- and upper-middle-class students and faculty from less well-off residents, responses to an incident or a conflictual situation can differ depending on who the parties are and the profile of the intervenor. In one midwestern community, a traffic accident caused by the negligent driving of a student attending one of the local universities resulted in the death of another student. Although the student offender was arrested and convicted on a criminal charge, many felt the penalty was comparatively light. Townspeople were quick to note that had a "townie" been the offender, the judge would have handed down a much more severe sentence.

If the definition of *community* is expanded to include state and local governments, the conflict potential is compounded. The political atmosphere in many jurisdictions has become increasingly conservative, and university officials have encountered resistance to university policy and procedures from local councils and state legislatures.

Given the fragility of university-community relationships, perhaps the more appropriate way to refer to the current state of affairs is "gown and frown" (Lewis, 1994). In this chapter, I look at town-and-gown conflicts through the lens of conflict analysis and resolution, providing insights into the nature of this conflict, and consider conflict resolution tools some universities are using and what more can be done.

Defining Town-and-Gown Conflicts

Town-and-gown conflicts are essentially community conflicts. As such, they have certain characteristics set out by Laue and Cormick (1978) in defining social conflict, which I have modified somewhat.

First, *they are multiparty disputes or conflicts.* Even what might appear to be a relatively minor dispute between noisy students in a rented house and next-door neighbors can quickly escalate to involve local police, university officials, parents, and lawyers depending on how the issue is defined and the investment of stakeholders in the outcome.

Second, *parties have different understandings of the origins of the conflict and the processes that should be used for dealing with it, and different expectations for outcomes.* One's perception of the origins of a conflict can be influenced by a number of factors, including culture, previous experiences with the parties to the conflict or experiences with this kind of conflict in some other locale, or some broader definition that may include actors who are in the background. The students in the above scenario may simply view this as a dispute with their neighbors. The neighbors, on the other hand, may view events as symptomatic of the way the university runs roughshod over local residents.

In turn, a party's sense of the origins of a conflict will likely influence how the party decides to process the conflict. By *process*, I refer to the approach a party will take in attempting to resolve a conflict in his or her favor. For example, if the students in question consider this an interpersonal dispute between them and their neighbors, we can assume their objective is to stay in the residence. They may want to choose a process of unassisted negotiations with the next-door neighbors or have the dispute mediated by a third party. If, on the other hand, the objective of their neighbors is to prevent this group of students (and to discourage any others) from living in the next-door residence, the neighbors may choose not to negotiate and may prefer a decisional option from an authoritative source brought about by arbitration or litigation. Of course, the situation becomes more complicated as more parties join the conflict.

A party's perspective on the origins of a conflict situation and the process chosen to respond to it shapes desired outcomes. Outcomes can be a consensual resolution, an imposed resolution by a decisional authority, or an escalation of the conflict. But outcomes can also speak to the product of a resolution. Moore (1986) identified three criteria necessary for the satisfactory resolution of disputes and conflicts: (1) Agreements usually have to acknowledge some *structural or substantive* concerns. In our students-neighbors conflict, this may mean the students agree to move an offending stereo to the other side of the house, away from the closest proximity to the neighbors, or to utilize an installation that can dampen sound. (2) There are occasions when *procedure*, how an agreement is implemented, will be an important ingredient to how satisfied parties feel. Students and their neighbors could work out an agreement on the kinds of music played at certain hours of the day. Students could agree to notify the neighbors when they intend to have a party, to place limitations on parking, and to control how participants conduct themselves at the party. (3) *Relationship* needs—how parties to an agreement feel they want to be treated— also must be addressed. In this case, students and neighbors could agree to engage in joint projects that relate to the upkeep of common areas of property or in a civic service that may have nothing to do with the immediate issues in the conflict.

Third, *the dispute or conflict occurs at and between different system levels.* By *system level,* I refer to the various interactive arenas in which the dispute or conflict can take place. Our students-neighbors issue can materialize as an interpersonal dispute, or it can take on a larger form as an organizational dispute. In the latter case, suppose the students are members of a fraternity that believes its members' rights are in danger of being abrogated, and that the fraternity is pitted against a neighborhood association whose members believe it is in the organization's interest to protect the rights of property owners. Finally, disputes can escalate to conflicts at the institutional level. Here, the university and its relevant policy actors, the city council, and the police department (which can be viewed as an organization and an institution) may weigh in to protect their interests. Obviously, the various systems in which the conflict can operate are not necessarily sequential.

Often, a conflict such as the one described can be taking place on various levels simultaneously. A helpful way of viewing this is to think of it as nested conflict (see Moira Dugan's model in Sandole and van der Merwe, 1993): The interpersonal is taking place within an organizational context, which, in turn, is embraced by interlocking institutional systems whose nexus is policy decisions that impact possible outcomes. This carries implications for the intervention process that is aimed toward consensual agreement. Careful assessment needs to be made as to the most appropriate level for intervention in order to maximize these outcomes. However, this is easier said than done. An intervention assessment may reveal several student-neighbor disputes incubating throughout the community. As such, the optimal intervention would be one that is viewed as fully integrative, that is, one that "increase[s] the total benefit available to the disputing parties through the search for creative solutions that satisfy their individual [and collective] interests" (Walton and McKersie, 1965). At this level, the process attempts to engage relevant policy and organizational actors to design a system that addresses root causes and goes beyond "cooling out" the conflict.

Fourth, *dispute or conflicts are of varying intensity, duration, and cost.* As implied from my earlier comments, intensity and duration of a conflict are affected by the level at which it is engaged. An unassisted negotiation resulting in an agreement could take as little as two or three hours at minimal cost, whereas a joint problem-solving process aimed toward a more holistic solution involving changes in patterns of behavior could take months and entail considerably more expense. The intensity of a conflict is heightened or lowered by how parties feel core values are being affected. Boulding (1962) called these "inner-core" values: unique epistemologies shaped by experiences of who we are, how we identify ourselves in the social universe, and how others respond to us in that universe. To the extent that parties feel these core values are threatened, they are likely to dig in their heels and fight.

Institutional Barriers to the Use of Alternative Dispute Resolution

Although I use the term *conflict analysis and resolution* to describe conflictual gown-and-gown relations, the more commonly used term is *alternative dispute resolution* (ADR). ADR describes various processes designed to resolve disputes and conflicts usually involving a third party. These approaches, ranging from informal problem-solving sessions where the third party's role is simply to facilitate discussion, to elaborate, multiparty consensus-building forums, have increasingly gained acceptance by individuals, courts of various jurisdictions, policymakers, and the private sector.

It must be recognized, however, that there are institutional barriers, still firmly in place, against using these techniques—and universities are no exception. The following are a few of the barriers that institutional officials throw up to block mediation (Bourne, n.d.): (1) *Mediation declares that the official is a failure at problem solving.* This seems to be particularly true at the midmanagerial level in administrative departments, where officials have built reputations around their ability to solve problems. The notion that a dispute or conflict is beyond their capability to resolve somehow threatens their image of themselves and their place in the hierarchy. (2) *By coming to the table, the individual abdicates his or her responsibility as a public official to make decisions.* This is the vested authority persona. The idea is that a manager or policymaker occupying a certain position has been given a mandate by the government (or governing board) to make decisions. To not do so, violates this mandate. (3) *Mediation empowers people one does not want to empower.* The status of conflictual arrangements is such that all outcomes are viewed through the lens of win-lose asymmetrical power. (4) *Mediation takes away one's ability to use a crisis to manage.* This is a variant of the first point where managers use crisis management to demonstrate their value to the institution. Indeed, in some organizations, managers invent crises as opportunities to manage. The mediation process could force a manager to move beyond a crisis to attend to long-term, underlying problems.

Mediation (or other forms of conflict resolution) at times can empower certain individuals and groups customarily removed from the decision-making arena. As well, mediation can penetrate the veneer of crisis management, leading to forms of long-term collaboration. In fact, a mediated process, skillfully conducted, can enhance a manager's power, make manifest his or her wisdom as a problem solver, and create new arenas for decision making and power sharing through the implementation of the agreement.

Applying a Preventive Model to Town-and-Gown Conflicts

The best system for resolving disputes and conflicts between universities and surrounding communities is to anticipate them and to put into place preventive mechanisms that attempt to deal with a problem before it reaches a boiling point. Recently, George Mason University, in Fairfax City, Virginia, purchased a group of townhouses as residences for faculty. Because George Mason is a state university, the townhouses were removed from the city's tax roll, further depleting the local treasury. While this action in and of itself might not have caused a conflict, it could very well have damaged relations in the long term. When another issue arose that may have been more conflictual on its face, the damaged relationships from the purchase of the townhouses could have migrated into the new situation.

Offsetting this, the university responded by providing an array of advisory services to the community. For example, a local road that passes on the periphery of the campus has become hazardous because of increased traffic and low visibility at certain points. Students volunteered to distribute literature throughout the community regarding traffic conditions. In addition, the university agreed to put in speed bumps at its own expense. To acknowledge this is a two-way street (pun intended), every year there is a mayor's service award to honor volunteer work that students perform for the community. It might appear at first sight that from a substantive standpoint the city got less than an equitable outcome. But in assessing trades explicit or implicit, we must measure satisfaction not in terms of mirror exchange but rather in terms of how parties *value* the trades.

Conclusion

In essence, the key to better town-and-gown relations is to move away from reactive forms of dispute resolution and toward anticipatory and preventive models. Universities should realize that they reside in ecologies of relationships that require open rather than closed systems of decision making. Other than strictly academic issues related to coursework and similarly narrow areas, all university policies should include, as part of their evaluation, consideration of what impact they will have on the surrounding community. The university can then reach out to local officials, bringing them into a dialogue to identify points of conflict and setting up a procedure for resolution. This process, called "partnering," is being used with increasing effectiveness to anticipate disputes that can arise between government and private contractors. In this form of dispute systems design, parties identify potentially conflictual issues and put in place gradually escalating forms of response ranging from unassisted negotiations to mediation by an outside third party, to arbitration, and, last (if necessary), to a decision by a power authority.

At George Mason's Institute for Conflict Analysis and Resolution, we emphasize the context in which the conflict takes place. It is our belief that most disputes or conflicts are part of a larger fabric of social interaction. While mediation can be applied at the microlevel of one-on-one disputes, sustainable resolution must take into consideration those factors that impact the disputants and the governance of the agreement. This does not mean we consider small-scale dispute resolution as *de minimis*. Many disputes need only a venue at this level to bring about a satisfactory and consensual resolution. We do urge that intervenors look at the larger context of the dispute and be alert for opportunities to transform the resolution to this arena. Implicitly, we believe that dispute resolution systems should address both the sources and consequences of conflict.

References

Boulding, K. E. *Conflict and Defense: A General Theory*. New York: HarperCollins, 1962.
Bourne, R. G. "Barriers to Mediation." Unpublished manuscript, Southeast Negotiation Network, College of Architecture, Georgia Institute of Technology, n.d.
Laue, J. H., and Cormick, G. "The Ethics of Social Intervention in Community Disputes." In G. Bermant and H. C. Kelman (eds.), *The Ethics of Social Intervention*. Washington, D.C.: Halsted Press, 1978.

Lewis, R. K. "When Town and University Relations Break Down." *Washington Post,* Dec. 12, 1994, p. E8.

Moore, C. W. *The Mediation Process: Practical Strategies for Resolving Conflict.* San Francisco: Jossey-Bass, 1986.

Sandole, D. J., and van der Merwe, H. (eds.). *Conflict Resolution Theory and Practice: Integration and Application.* Manchester, England: Manchester University Press, 1993.

Walton, R. E., and McKersie, R. B. *A Behavioral Theory of Labor Negotiations: An Analysis of a Social Interaction System.* New York: McGraw-Hill, 1965.

WALLACE WARFIELD is assistant professor and a member of the clinical faculty at the Institute for Conflict Analysis and Resolution, George Mason University, Fairfax, Virginia.

This chapter summarizes dispute resolution mechanisms used in various campus domains, organized roughly according to the degree of third-party influence and decision-making power involved.

Conflict Management in Higher Education: A Review of Current Approaches

William C. Warters

The following summary of conflict management mechanisms used in higher education is intended to provide readers with a good general overview of the field and a sense of some of the emergent trends. The work is informed by contacts developed in my role as chair of the Higher Education Committee of the National Association for Mediation in Education (NAME), and by the results of an exploratory study of conflict management in higher education (Holton and Warters, 1995) that surveyed the full range of campus services. Other valuable information sources include three national surveys of college-based campus mediation programs (Beeler, 1985; Warren, 1994; Warters and HeDeen, 1991), a national directory of law school mediation clinics (McDonald, 1994), a survey of university and college ombuds programs (Stern, 1990), and a national survey of student grievance handling procedures (Shubert and Folger, 1986). The mechanisms discussed are organized roughly according to the degree of third-party influence and decision-making power involved. High third-party power methods, such as the use of judicial boards or arbitration panels, are presented first, followed by a review of more informal and conciliatory approaches such as mediation.

Traditional Mechanisms for Handling Campus Conflict

In recent years there has been an increasing interest in campus conflict management approaches that come under the rubric of alternative dispute resolution. By way of discussing these alternative approaches, I look, first, at traditional mechanisms.

Resolving Disputes Involving Students. The range of dispute resolution approaches used with students has changed considerably over time, as colleges and universities have shifted their stance regarding student rights and responsibilities, and as the demographics of the student body has changed to include more adult learners. Until recently the trend in this area had been toward greater use of formal due process and courtlike procedures to ensure student rights and fend off possible litigation.

Student Conduct Committee Mechanisms. Prior to the 1960s, during the height of in loco parentis, few colleges and universities had clearly defined disciplinary action codes that provided students with a formal hearing and a process of appeal. However, in response to the student rights and student-as-consumer movement in the late 1960s and early 1970s, colleges and universities began to adopt codes of conduct and disciplinary procedures that more clearly and explicitly protected student rights. This trend was furthered by an increase in student-initiated litigation, and a series of federal regulations that specified guidelines for internal grievance hearings. All of these forces encouraged higher education institutions to provide more formalized mechanisms for resolving disputes internally.

Most colleges and universities now have detailed codes of conduct applicable to students. These conduct codes usually make a distinction between academic conduct issues and disciplinary conduct issues, providing somewhat different dispute resolution mechanisms for each. Academic conduct offenses that students may be charged with typically include issues such as cheating and plagiarism, which could ultimately warrant dismissal. Disciplinary conduct offenses often involve issues such as vandalism, violations of alcohol policies, harassment, and violations of noise policy. Alleged violators of college or university codes are required to participate in judicial proceedings initiated by the institution. These hearing processes vary somewhat in the degree to which they follow strict due process guidelines, depending on whether they take place in a public or private institution, and whether the offense is academic or disciplinary in nature.

Typically, student judicial processes begin with an opportunity for the student to admit responsibility for the conduct violation in a preliminary meeting with a designated administrative officer. The administrator then may assign a disciplinary action. If a student disagrees with the charges or the proposed sanction, the student usually is compelled to make his or her case in front of a panel of conduct board officers. These boards typically include specially trained representatives from both the administration and the student body, who together make a recommendation to the senior student affairs administrator regarding appropriate sanctions. The list of possible sanctions is often codified, and the board must pick from an approved list of options. In all of these processes, final decision-making authority usually remains with the senior administrator overseeing the academic or community conduct codes.

Student Grievance Systems. Students may also bring complaints against the college or university or its representatives. Grievances put forward by students may include charges of discrimination, sexual harassment, and capricious or arbitrary enactment of rules or regulations, and grievances about grades, the quality of instruction, the adequacy of financial aid awards, and many issues related to life in the residence hall. Colleges and universities have developed mechanisms to respond to these types of disputes as well. Shubert and Folger (1986) provide a good overview of student grievance systems. As they indicate, procedures to resolve these kinds of disputes typically involve three steps, the first requiring the student to make an attempt to resolve the dispute with whom it originated, the second bringing in a third party (with varying degrees of emphasis on adjudication or mediation), and the third step involving a final appeals mechanism through which the president or another high-ranking administrator makes a final determination.

Approaches to Resolving Conflicts Involving Faculty and Staff

In addition to resolving conflicts with their student "clients," colleges and universities have had to develop systems for resolving disputes among their employees, both faculty and staff. These conflicts are handled somewhat differently depending on whether it is a faculty or staff issue and whether or not a union is involved, but they often share common characteristics. They involve a range of issues, including complaints about rank or pay, dissatisfaction with status or classification, disagreements over assignments, problems concerning evaluation, problems concerning nonrenewal of contracts, problems concerning reprimands or censure, and charges of harassment or discrimination (Ludeman, 1989). If a complaint is not resolved using informal methods, it may become a formal grievance. Faculty grievance procedures tend to be fairly similar across different institutions and involve a predictable series of steps (McCarthy, Ladimer, and Sirefman, 1984). (Methods used to address staff disputes are usually quite similar to those employed in faculty disputes; these are not detailed separately here due to space constraints.)

Faculty Grievance Systems. Approximately one-third of the professoriat is represented by certified bargaining units in public and private, two- and four-year institutions (Douglas, 1989). Collectively bargained contracts typically specify what issues are grieveable. These contracts usually encourage administrators and employees to attempt to resolve problems before a grievance is filed. Once filed, there is commonly a series of three or four steps that must be followed: In the first step, the grievant presents his or her evidence in support of the grievance to a representative of the institution's administration, along with a proposed solution. The president or his or her representative must make a reply within a set period of time. If the issue cannot be resolved at this level, an internal or external review panel is set up to make an advisory recommendation to the administration and the grievant regarding a resolution. The final step in the process is usually arbitration, which is discussed briefly below.

When there is no union contract, the situation is handled differently. While almost all institutions, especially public ones, still provide due process procedures, they may be less rigorous. These procedures commonly involve one or more peer committees that deal with complaints. These committees may be appointed by administrators, chosen by senates, or elected at large. These committees hear charges, examine evidence, and keep records. They rarely have authority to change personnel decisions on their own. Typically, their charge is to make a recommendation to a high-level management representative, who then may or may not choose to follow the recommendation. If and when an employee has exhausted the internally set-out grievance procedures, the employee may then choose to take a case to trial if he or she feels that the decisions are unfair or capricious.

Arbitration. The majority of faculty collective bargaining agreements now have grievance systems that culminate in the use of arbitration. The arbitrator is employed to render a binding decision as the final step in the grievance system. The American Arbitration Association handles the bulk of these cases, with public relations employment boards and the Federal Mediation and Conciliation Service also used to a lesser extent (Douglas, 1989). An arbitrator's decision may be appealed to a court of law, but usually only on procedural issues, as the courts have shown considerable restraint on issues involving academic judgment and peer review.

Litigation. Colleges and universities have for years lamented the increased use of litigation as a dispute resolution mechanism, and the rising costs associated with this approach. Litigious responses to campus conflict represent the most adversarial approach on our continuum of intervention modes, and they challenge the cherished collegial image of the academic life. When colleges and universities are sued by students, staff, or faculty, cases tend to focus on issues related to allegations of arbitrary and capricious action, breach of contract, denial of constitutional rights, discriminatory practice, and unintentional or intentional breach of a common-law duty that resulted in injury to the individual. Tucker (1992) provides a useful review of the legal issues that college and university administrators may face, as well as patterns that can be gleaned from recent court cases.

Mediative or Conciliatory Mechanisms for Handling Campus Conflict

Now that we have examined the most common quasi-judicial approaches to resolving campus conflicts, we can turn our attention to the use of mediative or conciliatory methods, which have increased in popularity in recent years. Mediation involves a neutral third party (or parties, as many colleges use comediators or panels of mediators) who assists disputants in finding a mutually satisfactory resolution to their conflicts. While many mediation programs now serve multiple constituencies, for discussion purposes I address student-focused projects first, followed by faculty- and staff-oriented projects, and then those more clearly defined as multiconstituency.

Mediation of Student Disputes. Many student disputes involve other students or members of the local community. These disputes often involve parties who are interdependent, such as roommates, tenants and landlords, or dating couples, and they may focus on relationship concerns that do not in fact entail violation of any university policy. In the last fifteen years a trend has developed toward the increased use of mediation as a tool for resolving these types of student disputes (Warters, 1991), especially in cases that do not fit well within existing disciplinary mechanisms. Growth of these types of programs was propelled by the publication of *Peaceful Persuasion: A Guide to Creating Mediation Dispute Resolution Programs for College Campuses* (Girard, Townley, and Rifkin, 1985) and by a series of annual national conferences on campus mediation that began in 1990 at Syracuse University. This series of annual conferences has now merged with NAME, with that association's Committee on Higher Education as the sponsor.

Mediation programs are based in locations as diverse as counseling centers, ombuds offices, student government organizations, academic programs, research clinics, residential life programs, deans of students offices, campus judicial systems, off-campus housing offices, and student co-ops (Warters and HeDeen, 1991). The types of cases handled also vary widely, including student-student disputes (most often roommate cases), large group disputes, town-and-gown conflicts, sexual harassment cases, student-staff disputes, and even campus takeovers or shutdowns of campus buildings (Volpe and Witherspoon, 1992). Funding for centers varies greatly as well, with budgets ranging from pocket change to over $100,000 per year.

Based on a review of program survey results (Beeler, 1985; Shubert and Folger, 1986; Holton and Warters, 1995; Warters and HeDeen, 1991) and consultations with people starting new programs, my current estimate is that there are approximately one hundred college and university campuses in North America with distinct mediation projects in place to serve students, and the number is growing. Approximately two-thirds of these initiatives involve mediation centers or programs that have their own budgets and staff (albeit rather small). The other third represents mediation options that have been added to existing judicial systems without necessarily being designated as separate mediation programs. These figures do not include ombuds programs or mediation clinics based in law schools, which represent an additional, significant area of mediation work.

Mediation of Faculty Disputes. Most colleges and universities have established formal grievance systems for addressing disputes involving faculty. Many of these systems specifically build in steps known as "mediative efforts" wherein a panel of appointed faculty attempts to mediate a dispute by investigating the issues and working with parties in order to formulate an acceptable resolution. McCarthy, Ladimer, and Sirefman (1984) provide actual examples of grievance policies that include mediation steps. The American Association of University Professors also supports mediation and, in a given case, may involve representatives from its local chapter office, who after review of the case may assist in the mediation efforts.

Mediation of Staff Disputes. Many employee assistance programs regularly provide informal conciliation services, as do university and college ombuds offices. Specialized mediation services for employee conflicts seem to be growing in number as well. Most of these projects are relatively new and usually involve the training of a core group of staff who are then available to mediate disputes. New techniques are being tested in this area to address the influence of workplace cultures and hierarchical structures on maintaining agreements after mediation.

Ombuds Programs. Perhaps the most enduring and successful multiple-constituency model for resolving campus conflicts is the college ombudsperson. The ombuds role emerged on North American campuses in the late 1960s. Although the early programs primarily handled student complaints, the majority of offices today have expanded their focus to include the handling of faculty, staff, and administrative problems as well (Stern, 1990).

An ombuds program is specifically designed to handle conflict situations through a combination of fact finding, mediation, and conciliation. By the very nature of the office, the ombudsperson does not exercise any administrative powers. He or she is not in a position to command behavior of administrative officials or faculty members, or to reverse their decisions. Instead, the powers of the office are derived from the ombud's authority to access administrative records and files, to investigate policies and decisions against which grievances have been registered, to negotiate among parties involved for an agreeable settlement of the problem, and, when warranted, to publicize certain patterns of conflict so as to facilitate change in policy and procedure.

Off-Campus Services. An interesting extension of the growth of campus dispute resolution initiatives has been the development of a host of projects that reach beyond the campus walls. Some of these programs focus on landlord-tenant disputes and are affiliated with the off-campus housing offices, while others are jointly sponsored with local municipalities. Other campus projects work to smooth town-and-gown relations through proactive problem-solving meetings with neighbors in problematic neighborhoods.

Another important outreach effort involves college and university mediation programs working in collaboration with local elementary and secondary schools and community colleges to develop and support peer mediation and conflict resolution training programs at other levels of the education system. A third increasingly common model involves law school mediation clinics staffed by law students in training. A recent roster developed by the American Association of Law Schools Alternative Dispute Resolution Section (McDonald, 1994) lists more than thirty law schools that currently have or are developing mediation clinics that mediate cases referred from local courts or police.

While most of these programs work strictly with court-referred cases, some programs are offering specialized services for conflicts arising within city housing projects or other community settings.

Trends in the Field

As alternative dispute resolution work on college campuses develops, a number of trends are emerging that signal a maturation of the field. These include the development of various dispute resolution consortiums, such as the Colorado Conflict Resolution Consortium and Clearinghouse (based at the University of Colorado) and the new City University of New York Dispute Resolution Consortium. In a similar vein, a resolution to support and encourage alternative methods of dispute resolution was recently passed by the Board of Regents of the University of Georgia, and a blue-ribbon committee was established to bring forward recommendations for the enhancement of alternative dispute resolution methods for students, faculty, and staff across Georgia's entire state system of thirty-four institutions.

In addition to these larger-scale organizing efforts, there is also increased use of internet discussion groups such as CCRNET (campus conflict resolution network) as a networking tool among campus dispute resolvers, and there are now regional meetings of campus mediation programs to supplement annual national gatherings. There is increasing availability of college and university conflict resolution training for staff and faculty, and a growing emphasis on preparing campus mediators to handle more complex conflicts involving issues of culture, race, and gender. Some programs are also now moving beyond interpersonal disputes and are beginning to intervene in larger group conflicts involving various campus constituencies. There is also the continuing spread of mediation techniques to previously undeveloped areas such as community colleges and local communities. Finally, there appears to be a gradual move toward institutionalization of mediation as a preferred mode of dispute resolution on campus, signified by the gradual development of campus grievance policies that include mediation in their basic procedures.

Conclusion

Clearly, there has been considerable growth and development in the area of campus conflict resolution. We need as well a comparable increase in the research on and documentation of campus dispute resolution efforts, and a refinement and integration of campus dispute resolution systems. While the ivory tower will never be free of conflict, it certainly has the potential to become one of the most well managed areas of conflict activity, wherein the true value of conflict can be discovered, and the painful costs of conflict poorly handled can be minimized.

References

Beeler, K. D. *Institutions with Identified Conflict-Resolution (Mediation) Programs*. Charleston: Eastern Illinois University, 1985.

Douglas, J. "Arbitration in Academe." *National Center for the Study of Collective Bargaining in Higher Education and the Professions Newsletter,* 1989, 17 (2), 1–7.

Girard, K., Townley, A., and Rifkin, J. *Peaceful Persuasion: A Guide to Creating Mediation Dispute Resolution Programs for College Campuses*. Amherst, Mass.: The Mediation Project, 1985.

Holton, S. A, and Warters, W. C. *National Survey on Conflict Management in Higher Education*. Bridgewater, Mass.: Bridgewater State College, 1995.

Ludeman, R. B. "The Formal Academic Grievance Process in Higher Education: A Survey of Current Practices." *NASPA Journal,* 1989, 2 (3), 235–240.

McCarthy, J., Ladimer, I., and Sirefman, J. P. *Managing Faculty Disputes: A Guide to Issues, Procedures, and Practices*. San Francisco: Jossey-Bass, 1984.

McDonald, C. B. *ADR Clinic Directory (Law Schools)*. Malibu, Calif.: Pepperdine University, 1994.

Shubert, J. J., and Folger, J. P. "Research Report: Learning from Higher Education." *Negotiation Journal,* 1986, 2 (4), 395–406.

Stern, L. "1990 Ombudsperson Survey." *University and College Ombuds Association Newsletter,* Fall 1990, p. 5.

Tucker, A. "Legal Implications of Being a Chair." In A. Tucker (ed.), *Chairing the Academic Department: Leadership Among Peers*. (3rd ed.) New York: American Council on Education/Macmillan, 1992.

Volpe, M., and Witherspoon, R. "Mediation and Cultural Diversity on College Campuses." *Mediation Quarterly,* 1992, 9 (4), 341–351.

Warren, B. *Survey of College/University Mediation Services*. Bloomington: Indiana University, 1994.

Warters, B. "Mediation on Campus: A History and Planning Guide." *The Fourth R: Newsletter of the National Association of Mediation in Education,* 1991, 33, 4–5.

Warters, B., and HeDeen, T. *Campus-Based Mediation Programs Survey*. Syracuse, N.Y.: Syracuse University, 1991.

WILLIAM C. WARTERS *is assistant professor in the Department of Dispute Resolution at Nova Southeastern University, Fort Lauderdale, Florida, and chair of the Higher Education Committee of the National Association for Mediation in Education.*

What do we look for? How do we understand, analyze, and work with the conflict that confronts academics every day? This chapter describes specific tools for analyzing, understanding, and managing conflict.

And Now . . . the Answers! How to Deal with Conflict in Higher Education

Susan A Holton

Conflict is inevitable in higher education, where academic freedom is revered and free thinking is encouraged. It is vital that we understand the conflicts that occur in higher education, and that we learn to deal effectively with them. Lack of understanding of conflict leads to an inability to cope with it. "Inability to cope with conflict constructively and creatively leads to increased hostility, antagonism, and divisiveness; clear thinking disintegrates, and prejudice and dogmatism come to prevail. This is the antithesis of the university norm of 'reasoned discourse' " (Blake, Mouton, and Williams, 1981, p. 5).

Early Warning Signs

Conflict is often subtle and creeps into a situation without conscious awareness. It is thus important to know the early warning signs of conflict. Gmelch and Carroll (1991) identified ten structural relationships that can create conflict: organizational levels, degree of authority, degree of specialization, staff composition, nature of supervision, participation in decision making, sources of power, rewards and recognition, interdependence among working units, and roles and responsibilities. They discovered that as institutions grow and the organizations become more complex, conflict is likely to increase: "As the size of the institution increases, goals become less clear, interpersonal relationships more formal, departments more specialized, and the potential for conflict intensifies" (Gmelch and Carroll, 1991, p. 109).

NEW DIRECTIONS FOR HIGHER EDUCATION, no. 92, Winter 1995 © Jossey-Bass Publishers

Degrees of authority are often unclear in academic institutions. For faculty, who usually have significant autonomy, "the potential for interpersonal conflict increases since roles and expectations become less clear and more difficult to monitor and supervise" (Gmelch and Carroll, 1991, p. 109).

Within departments, the degree of homogeneity leads to more constructive conflict. "Established groups have been found to develop more constructive conflict than *ad hoc* committees, thus as tenure of group members increases, conflict is more likely to be functional; stability may be a factor in increased constructive departmental conflicts" (Gmelch and Carroll, 1991, p. 110). The converse is that frequent turnover in departments or divisions leads to greater conflict.

The degree of supervision in an institution of higher education depends on the groups; faculty are often loosely supervised and staff may be highly supervised. Gmelch and Carroll found that the closer one is supervised, the more frequently conflict is created.

Sources of power within higher education differ depending on the role that one plays. In examining conflict, Gmelch and Carroll found that the use of expertise and referent power (personal sources) yields greater satisfaction and performance of staff than does coercive power.

The issue of inadequate fiscal resources leads to conflict within higher education today. Gmelch and Carroll found that rewards and recognition contribute significantly to conflict; the more rewards emphasize separate performance rather than combined performance, the greater the conflict. "Faculty, who mostly teach in isolation, naturally find themselves in competition for and in conflict over the limited resources for reward and recognition" (Gmelch and Carroll, 1991, p. 120). This problem is also reflected in the relationship of interdependence, where the limitation of resources is seen as a zero-sum game. Often, faculty and others on campus see that the allocation of resources to one individual, department, or division means that another will receive nothing. Hence, conflict occurs.

The ambiguity of faculty and administrator roles is the final element in the structural relationships within academia. Because the two roles are organized differently, operated differently, and have different cultures, conflict is inevitable.

Given these structural relationships that can cause conflict, it is surprising that we do not have *more* conflict in higher education!

A Conflict Model

While it may appear that conflict emerges overnight, there is actually a distinct process that can be identified in most conflicts. Filley's (1975) six-element model of conflict is an accurate reflection of the conflict process: (1) antecedent conditions, (2) perceived conflict or (3) felt conflict, (4) manifest behavior, (5) conflict resolution or suppression, and (6) resolution aftermath.

Antecedent conditions are the characteristics of a situation that generally lead to conflict, although they may be present in the absence of conflict as well. As reflected in this concept of antecedent condition, and that of resolution aftermath, conflict *management* is a more accurate term than conflict *resolution*. Every conflict leaves the parties with an interactional history that will influence future contact. So conflict is rarely fully resolved, but it is often managed well.

According to Levinger and Rubin (1994), there are three types of antecedent conditions: (1) physical context of conflict (site location, communication opportunities, time limits, and so on), (2) social context (number of disputants, openness of the conflict site to various observers or third-party interveners, aspects of the disputant's relationship, individual expectations, personality considerations, and so on), and (3) issue context (the number of issues in dispute, their sequencing, packaging, and so on). Imbalance in any one of these antecedent conditions can lead to conflict, either perceived or felt.

Filley (1975) distinguished between logical and emotional or personal conflict. He defined perceived conflict as a logically and impersonally recognized set of conditions that are conflictive to the parties; on a parallel track is felt conflict, personalized conflict relationship, expressed in feelings of threat, hostility, fear, and mistrust.

In support of the concept of felt conflict, Merry and Sibley (1984) concluded that dispute behavior is affective and habitual and is not entirely a matter of rational calculation; much behavior is also unconscious and this too may be rational or nonrational. "Our data suggest that much dispute behavior continues to be governed by affect, habit, and conceptions of right, appropriateness, or fittingness that are not subject to rational evaluation but are part of the taken-for-granted quality of daily life in particular communities" (Merry and Sibley, 1984, p. 158).

Action, or manifest behavior, is always construed as a result of perceived or felt conflict. The types of conflict responses, or manifest behavior, are explicated by Blake and Mouton's (1970) conflict management grid (see Figure 11.1). The conflict response is based on concern for people (cooperativeness or supportive and nonsupportive) and concern for production of results (assertive, submissive and dominant). This 2-by-2 grid gives five distinct styles of manifest behavior: avoidance, accommodation, collaboration, and competition, with the fifth middle ground of compromise (Blake and Mouton, 1964).

Finally, the parties involved in conflict bring it to a conclusion through conflict resolution or suppression. How they do that varies greatly depending on the parties, the conflict, and the context. The level of conflict also determines the appropriate resolution or management of the conflict. Sometimes conflict is suppressed instead. While that may be an immediate solution, the conflict will always resurface, often more intensely.

What happened as a result of the agreements made among colleagues after the last budget cut? Do they still remember? That is the resolution aftermath. It is this phase that reinforces the reality that conflict is not completely resolved

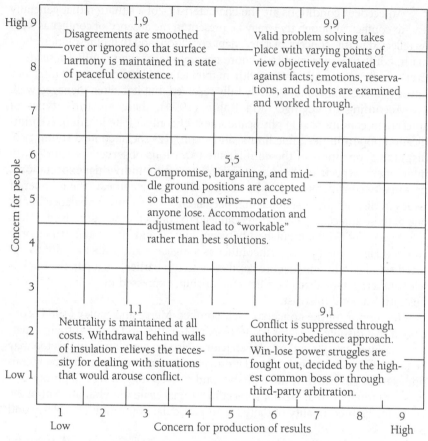

Figure 11.1. Conflict Management Grid

Source: R. R. Blake and J. S. Mouton, "The Fifth Achievement," *Journal of Applied Behavioral Science,* 6 (4), 413–426, copyright © 1970 by Sage Publications. Reprinted by permission of Sage Publications, Inc.

but rather is managed. There is always an aftermath of the resolution of conflict. It may be positive, as members of a department or division learn to work effectively together and draw on that goodwill for the next conflict. Or it may be negative, as the "losers" in the conflict vow never to cooperate with the "winners." Conflict patterns are perpetuated and conflicts often become a cause for disputants. The conflict often becomes cyclical. Conflict often reflects patterned behavior and is predictable. Especially in groups, such as departments or divisions, where the same people interact over many years, repeated conflict patterns are likely to occur.

It is important to understand the process of conflict. If the same conflict continually occurs in a department, it may be valuable to look at the conflict aftermath and see whether the conflict has ever really been resolved or managed. If some conflict seems "overly emotional," it is important to look at the aspects of perceived and felt conflict. Each area of Filley's model is valuable in understanding the conflict as it occurs in the institution, or for analyzing the conflict after it has been managed.

Holton Model of Conflict Management

Once the process of conflict is understood, it is important to learn how to manage it. The Holton Model of Conflict Management analyzes the three parts of the conflict management process: identification of conflict, identification of solutions, and implementation of these solutions.

Probably the most important aspect of this model is listening. In order to understand a conflict, one must listen intensely to all involved in the conflict. Too often, there is a rush to resolve the conflict before full attention has been paid to all of the people and the issues. The result is that perhaps one aspect of the conflict, usually the most easily identifiable aspect, is worked on. And the root of the conflict is left to grow again.

No steps of this model should be left out. To leave one out is to ignore one possibly significant piece in the puzzle that is conflict.

Identify the Conflict. The identification phase of conflict management is a six-step process. All of the steps are necessary to understanding the conflict.

1. *Who is involved?*
   Identify all of the parties who are involved in the conflict, and all who are not (which may be just as important as one tries to understand the conflict).
   What is the relationship of those who are involved? In what ways are they interdependent? Has their relationship changed? What are their roles and responsibilities in relationship to one another and to this conflict situation? What prior interactions have occurred among those in conflict? Have they been adversaries before? Is this a new conflict? Do they trust one another? Are they polarized?
   What are the motivations of those involved in the conflict? What do they say are their goals and objectives? How does their behavior support or negate claims?
   What are the sources of power of those in conflict?
   Who are the people not directly involved in the conflict but likely to be affected by it? Who are those who are likely to be brought into the conflict if it escalates?
2. *What is the conflict?*
   What happened? What are the specific, observable data about the conflict?
   What are the feelings and emotions surrounding the conflict? What are the presenting issues? What are the secondary (tertiary and so on) issues?

3. *When did it happen?*
   When did the conflict begin? Is there a specific incident that can be identified? Is it ongoing? Is it cyclical? Is it intermittent?
   Does it escalate or die down?
4. *Where did it happen?*
   Where physically did the conflict occur? Where, within the organizational structure, did it occur?
5. *Resolution attempts?*
   What attempts have been made to manage the conflict? If it is a recurring conflict, what attempts have been made in the past? In what ways were those attempts successful? In what ways were they not?
6. *Consequences of the conflict?*
   What will happen if the conflict is not resolved? What will happen if it is? What gains and losses are perceived to exist as a result of solutions?

After this information about the nature of the conflict has been acquired, the conflict can be understood. Then it is necessary to work with the parties directly involved in the conflict to identify solutions. Those directly involved in the conflict must work together (often with a neutral third party) to identify solutions.

Identify Solutions. The development of solutions is not a simple process. Setting the stage and getting parties to communicate and work together is a necessary part of this phase of the conflict management process.

1. *Develop a positive attitude.* Unless those involved in a conflict are willing to work together toward a mutually agreeable solution, no management is possible. And so the first step is to work with the parties to develop a positive attitude. This may require a discussion about ways in which the parties might benefit from working together in the future, and about the positive outcomes that are possible as a result of the management of this conflict.
2. *Establish ground rules.* Conflict often produces feelings of chaos. It is therefore important to work with the parties to establish ground rules for the conflict management. A part of those ground rules may be the identification of the communication expectations. A quick lesson in active listening and giving and receiving feedback may help parties to communicate more effectively in the process of the conflict management. Also, it is reassuring to have structure for the management of the conflict. Parties should agree, at the beginning of the process, on specific times and locations (preferably neutral territory) for the meetings. It is also vitally important that everyone agree to attend all meetings until the conflict is resolved.
3. *Identify interests of the parties.* Parties must understand their priorities, and the outcome or outcomes they want. Fisher and Ury (1981) wrote extensively about the importance of interests versus positions. Parties need to understand what they truly want as a result of the management of the

conflict. This includes an understanding of what Fisher and Ury (1981) referred to as the best alternative to the negotiated agreement, or BATNA. Sometimes it helps to explain to parties what will happen if they do not come together to manage the conflict. Often the threat of externally imposed solutions is enough to get parties to agree to work together.

4. *Develop alternatives.* Now that the issues of the conflict are understood, it is important to identify alternative solutions for managing it. Brainstorming is the best process to develop alternatives. In an environment of trust (usually facilitated by the neutral third party) disputants can work together to develop multiple alternatives. It is also helpful to identify ways that similar issues have been managed in other situations. Such background gives the disputants an acknowledgment that solutions are possible, and it may expand their concepts of possible alternatives. It is important that this phase be kept separate from the decision making based on criteria.

5. *Identify criteria.* Not all of the ideas generated during the previous stage will be appropriate for the individual conflict. It is then necessary to identify appropriate criteria and to use those criteria to determine the "best" solutions. First, there are often objective criteria, given the nature of the conflict. These may include such issues as time (must be resolved by the end of the semester) or money (must not cost more than $1,000). Some criteria are also subjective (Will the trustees like it?). These are often overlooked, to the peril of the conflict management. After the criteria have been developed, they should be prioritized; not all criteria will carry equal weight in the decision making.

6. *Weigh solutions against criteria.* The solutions should be weighed against the prioritized criteria, and a "best solution" will result. It is important to determine whether that solution is, in fact, felt to be the best by all parties. Too often, after a solution has been determined, parties realize that they left out important criteria. They may, for example, have identified only rational, logical criteria and ignored emotional aspects of the decision. Or they may agree on a solution but realize that they do not have the time to implement it.

Implement the Solutions. Too often, this is the phase of conflict management that is neglected. Even when significant time is spent on identification of the conflict and identification of potential solutions, the implementation phase is often rushed. And it cannot be. To have successful conflict management, the parties must be diligent about the implementation phase.

1. *Develop a plan of action.* It is not enough to agree to a nebulous solution; all parties in the conflict must agree to the specifics of the solution. The plan of action should include the following: First, who is going to be involved in the implementation of the solutions? If some people outside the immediate system of the parties are involved, how are they going to

be brought in to the solution phase? Second, what *exactly* is to be done? Be as specific as possible about the actions that are to be taken. Third, when are the parties going to act? Develop a very clear and concise time line. What is going to be done tomorrow? By what date will the complete solution be in place? What checkpoints do the parties have along the way? Fourth, include "check in" dates in the time line, when the parties will get together to talk about the solution and the progress that is being made, and to work with any issues that arise during the implementation phase. Fifth, who is responsible for mediating differences among the parties during the implementation phase? The plan of action should be written up and signed by all parties, including the neutral third party if one is involved. This document will be more valuable if every aspect of the agreement is clearly spelled out in terms that will not be debatable in the future.

2. *Determine how to handle conflict in the future.* As part of the conflict management process, the parties should agree on a way to deal with conflict in the future. They may, for example, agree to go to the university ombuds officer, to appoint a conflict management committee, or to meet monthly to discuss issues and avert problems.

Following this process will be time-consuming. But anyone who has been involved in a conflict knows how much time and energy is consumed by conflict. This model not only deals with the conflict but also provides a way to deal with conflict in the future. In the long run, time is saved.

It is also important to note that as soon as one begins this process of conflict management, the conflict dynamics will change. The "simple" act of listening to people starts the process of conflict management.

Levels of Conflict

Not all conflicts are the same. With some conflicts, parties would rather label the trouble a mild disagreement over semantics; with others, it is seen as a zero-sum game where one needs to win, at the expense of the other; and sometimes conflict is accurately described as a war. Too often, all conflict is grouped together. People hear the word *conflict* and immediately think of a war. In reality, there are many levels of conflict.

To accurately analyze and deal with conflict, it is necessary to understand the levels of conflict. The appropriate intervention for one level is different from that for another level. Some conflicts require actions that can be worked out between the parties, others necessitate the intervention of a third party.

Donohue and Kolt (1992) identified seven levels of conflict and tension: no conflict, latent conflict, problems to solve, dispute, help, fight or flight, and intractable. I supply the suggested interventions.

Level 1: No Conflict. The parties face no key differences in goals. At this level, the parties need to have clear, productive communication and need to be free to address their differences. Is this level healthy? Certainly it is if the parties discuss the conflict. It can also be a screen for further conflicts. But if the parties use it as a way to evade conversation, then this level is not productive.

This level is also referred to as "pseudo conflict," which is really conflict that results from unsuccessful communication exchanges. The three causes of pseudo conflict are semantic difficulties, insufficient exchange of information, and noise; these lead to unsuccessful exchange of information, which leads to pseudo conflict (Rhenman, Stromberg, and Westerlund, 1974).

The intervention strategy at this level is to get the parties to sit down and have a productive conversation, and to ensure that they understand one another. Clear definition of the problem is very important here; the parties cannot hope to resolve the conflict if they cannot define the issues to mutual satisfaction. No outsider is needed here; the parties can identify that there is a misunderstanding and work to correct it.

Level 2: Latent Conflict. In this level of conflict, one person senses a problem and believes there are goal differences; however, the other does not notice the differences or denies that they exist. With this level, it is important that the person who perceives the conflict discuss it with the other party. The intervention may be as simple as getting the two people to sit down to talk and agree on a definition of the problem. The difficulty is that if one does not see a conflict, he or she may not see the need to talk. Even at this level of conflict, it may be helpful to have a third party (perhaps a colleague or peer) facilitate the communication process. If the conflict is ignored, then the person who perceives the conflict may feel devalued and may let the conflict grow in his or her mind.

Level 3: Problems to Solve. At this level, the people in conflict realize that there are issues. Here they are able to focus on interests and do not have the goal to attack the other or to save face. At Level 3, the conflict is seen by both parties as a problem to solve; they are willing to share information and to work together.

At this level, it is possible to bring the parties together to share the problem and to mutually solve it. It is recommended that an outside person help the parties define the problem and the solutions, but this facilitator can be a third party within the institution, as in Level 2.

Level 4: Dispute. Whereas Level 3 is problem-centered, Level 4 includes the need-centered dimension. The conflict is described as need-centered, but personal attacks enter, bringing the conflict into a destructive mode. At this level, personal needs take precedence over the problem. People want to first protect themselves—the problem is secondary.

Third-party intervention is vital. While this third party can often be someone on campus, the individual should not be someone who might be involved, either currently or historically, in the conflict. This person also must have the trust of both (all) parties involved.

It is important at this level to talk to both parties to determine the facts, both the "feeling" facts and the objective facts. No one will work on solving the problems unless the needs are acknowledged. These needs may not be totally met, but it is important that they be acknowledged and that each party hears about the needs of the other.

Level 5: Help. At this level, the parties realize that they can no longer manage their dispute because they are out of control (possibly with personal needs-centered issues). Sometimes the individuals have tried to manage the dispute themselves; frequently, they have enlisted the aid of others. As a part of this level, the groups form sides, enlisting others outside the conflict.

A third party is definitely needed here. The parties involved need to be able to communicate but will be reluctant to do so. If they have tried to manage the conflict, and failed, they wonder if it can be solved. A third party from outside the system needs to come in to establish firm ground rules, take over the guidance of the conflict solution phase, and earn the confidence of the parties. With that confidence, the third party can begin to get the parties to talk with each other, to reveal their interests, and to develop ways to manage the conflict.

Level 6: Fight or Flight. Anger is the prime emotion at this level of conflict. The parties declare battle; they strategize about how to destroy each other. Usually, each party at this level does not wish to escape but wants the other to leave. This level of conflict is highly emotional. People enlist the aid of others, feeling that it is important for everyone to be on their side. If someone attempts to remain neutral, he or she is seen as a part of the enemy camp.

As with Level 5, it is mandatory that outside help be brought in to work with the parties. In addition to the matters mentioned above in the management of Level 5, it is important in Level 6 to give the parties time to speak individually to the neutral party. In this level, it is vitally important to listen to the personal needs of the parties, and to help them work through those needs to understand their own interests and those of the other parties. It is difficult, and important, to work with the parties to restore civil conversation, and to restore or develop levels of trust and respect.

Level 7: Intractable. Not all conflict can be managed in a way that maintains the status quo. Especially when a conflict has gone on for a long time, it develops a life of its own. Parties invest much energy in sustaining the conflict and that becomes more important than conflict resolution. At this level of conflict, parties talk negatively, to anyone who will listen, including the press, about the conflict and about the "enemy." Parties involved see themselves as "doing the right thing." Their cause is to bring justice to the situation, not just to defeat the enemy. Each side, of course, sees his or hers as the "just" one.

Not all conflicts are the same. It is inappropriate to deal with conflicts as if they were the same. Obviously, it is best to catch the conflict and deal with it at the lowest level possible. There is no specific timing to the escalation of conflict; some conflicts escalate like a grease fire and others smolder with few visible embers for years. But the best way to deal with conflict is to recognize it, work to understand it, and manage it as soon as it is visible.

Conclusion

Conflict can no longer be ignored within the ivory tower. In order to deal with conflict effectively, it is necessary to be aware of the structural relationships that often call forth conflict—and to watch those relationships for signs of trouble. It is important to understand the antecedent conditions of conflict and, again, to watch those conditions for early signs of conflict. The earlier a conflict is identified, the easier it is to manage and the less expensive it is in terms of personnel and resources. A conflict left unmanaged will only grow and bring increasing hardship to the individuals, the departments, and the institutions. The metaphor of cancer is often used to describe this level of conflict; the cancer must be eradicated or it will take over the host department, division, and even institution.

References

Blake, R. R., and Mouton, J. S. *The Managerial Grid.* Houston: Gulf, 1964.

Blake, R. R., and Mouton, J. S. "The Fifth Achievement." *Journal of Applied Behavioral Science,* 1970, *6* (4), 413–426.

Blake, R. R., Mouton, J. S., and Williams, M. S. *The Academic Administrator Grid: A Guide to Developing Effective Management Teams.* San Francisco: Jossey-Bass, 1981.

Donohue, W. A, and Kolt, R. *Managing Interpersonal Conflict.* Thousand Oaks, Calif.: Sage, 1992.

Filley, A. C. *Interpersonal Conflict Resolution.* Glenview, Ill.: Scott, Foresman, 1975.

Fisher, R., and Ury, W. *Getting to Yes: Negotiating Agreement Without Giving In.* Boston: Houghton Mifflin, 1981.

Gmelch, W. H., and Carroll, J. B. "The Three Rs of Conflict Management for Department Chairs and Faculty." *Innovative Higher Education,* 1991, *16* (2), 107–123.

Levinger, G., and Rubin, J. Z. "Bridges and Barriers to a More General Theory of Conflict." *Negotiation Journal,* 1994, *10,* 201–215.

Merry, S. E., and Sibley, S. S. "What Do Plaintiffs Want? Reexamining the Concept of Dispute." *Justice System Journal,* 1984, *9* (2), 151–178.

Rhenman, E., Stromberg, L., and Westerlund, G. In S. P. Robbins (ed.), *Managing Organizational Conflict: A Nontraditional Approach.* Englewood Cliffs, N.J.: Prentice Hall, 1974.

SUSAN A HOLTON *is professor of communication studies at Bridgewater State College, Bridgewater, Massachusetts, and director of the Massachusetts Faculty Development Consortium.*

What is the future of conflict in higher education? What needs to be done to ensure that conflict can be a positive, constructive experience in the academy?

Where Do We Go from Here?

Susan A Holton

Conflict will not disappear from the academy, nor should it. There are those who argue that it is a necessary component of change within the academy. Conflict can be a positive force in higher education. Conflict can be cathartic, providing opportunities for revitalization, energizing, and creativity by all involved in the academy.

Conflict in higher education is clearly more pronounced today. That may be because of the changes that have taken place. According to Donna Shavlik of the American Council on Education, "Conflict in higher education is greater than ever before, more hostile. It has to do with our inability to think about a way in which we can enlarge our paradigm—who is included and isn't, who is important and isn't, who belongs and doesn't. When we have a narrow view, we eliminate the ability to enlarge the organization and we get contentious. The changes in higher education over the past few years make conflict management more necessary. We need conflict to challenge, engage, sharpen and need to do it with some rules of engagement, not brutal personal attacks; need to do it with respect and understanding" (personal communication, March 23, 1995). Higher education must learn to manage conflict, to take the new realities of academic life and forge a positive, constructive approach to conflict management.

Change in higher education will continue to intensify conflict, and the need for people who know how to manage conflict. "Progress and change cannot be made without conflict, and nothing is more important for American higher education than the emergence of academic leaders equipped to handle the conflicts created by these challenges" (Gmelch and Carroll, 1991, p. 107).

However, as we face these changes, it is vital to learn ways to deal with the conflicts. "The challenge is to create vehicles for dealing with conflict in an environment that is open to differences. Indeed, a characteristic of many successful campuses has been the creation of strong policies, procedures and even special programs of mediation and arbitration to recognize the existence of conflict and to use it as a vehicle for learning by the institution" (Green, 1990, p. 12).

In order to cope with the changes in higher education, and with the conflicts that will always be a part of the academy, strong leadership is needed. "We need strong leaders, with honesty and candor who work with consensus building. Leadership is the key variable in making things possible. Unfortunately, there are few places for them to learn that" (Parker Palmer, personal communication, March 14, 1995).

Leadership Challenges

Higher education must develop leaders within all sectors of the academy who can deal with change and conflict. For years there have been a few programs that train leaders in higher education; most prominent are the Higher Education Resource Service Summer Institute for Women at Bryn Mawr and the Management Development Program and Institute for Educational Management at Harvard University. Today, however, leadership development is emerging as a priority on campuses. McDade and Lewis (1994) present a variety of models of leadership development programs, from campus-based to externships. According to Robert Diamond, an administrator and scholar who has studied the changes in higher education, "We are at a point where so severe is the need for change that we have to do it, we are beginning to know what we must change. The key is to develop the leadership that knows how to lead change" (personal communication, March 20, 1995).

Leaders—current and potential—must be trained to deal with the realities of change and conflict. Perhaps no skill is more important. The cry for leadership in higher education must be heard, and those leaders must be trained in conflict management. As McCarthy (1980) noted,

> The way administrators handle conflict has a pronounced influence on how the institution is viewed, both within the college and in the larger community. If administrators believe that conflict is an unwarranted intrusion into the smooth running of the institution, they become annoyed and impatient with demands and tend to procrastinate in responding to grieving faculty members. This apparent insensitivity fosters an impression of institutional intransigence. If, however, administrators see conflict as a natural and even healthy aspect of their relationship with the faculty, they will be responsible to faculty concerns and demonstrate the institution commitment to thoughtful and thorough consideration of issues within a rational problem-solving framework.

Cultural Challenges

In addition to the development of leaders who can manage conflicts, we need also to acknowledge problems within the culture of higher education that exacerbate the conflicts. We need, therefore, to develop forums for dealing with conflict and culture.

Very few institutions have such forums. It is vital for all members of the campus community to have input in decisions. That may lessen the conflict, as people who are involved with decision making are less likely to fight the ensuing changes. But, clearly, more forums are needed to address problems. Parker Palmer (personal communication, March 14, 1995) observes that "one of the problems of academic culture is that it is too privatized, there are few public forums to bring conflict. There is a voicelessness in faculty; they are afraid to speak up, afraid that they will be shot down. . . . What we need is open, honest discourse. That may begin by talking about the deep pain that is present in higher education . . . then talk about the ways in which each one is responsible for our own pain. We need to name the realities of pain, isolation, disconnectedness. We need to look at what is the root disease, and what are the cures."

Within higher education we need a culture that supports and acknowledges a systemic view of conflict, a view that acknowledges that conflict within one part of the academy has an effect on all other parts. As systems theory purports, change and conflict permeate the entire system. And so dealing with the conflict will require an engagement of all elements of the system and a cultural shift for most institutions of higher education.

Development of Community

Academics, like others in society at large, often pine for a long lost utopia. But it has been argued that the "good old days" never were, that there is a false sense of what the academic community used to be like. What we need is not a return to the nostalgia of Camelot but a new sense of community, encompassing everyone on campus.

And the time is certainly ripe for the development of academic community. Parker Palmer, who has been most vocal in his advocacy of community, suggests that the problem may be one of past affluence: "When institutions are fat and happy, as higher education was for a number of years, community tends not to happen, because there's more than enough to go around and people can retreat into privatism and still get their slice of the pie. Then there's a curve of declining resources in institutions during which people start discovering each other and their need for each other. . . . I see more and more people coming out of privatized academic lives into various forms of academic community—forums, working parties, open-ended conversations—motivated in part by dwindling dollars" (Edgerton, 1992, p. 4). Other educators agree. Michael Hooker, president of the University of North Carolina at Chapel Hill, argued that "the greatest challenge to us on campus today is to reestablish a sense of community. . . . I sense today a growing spirit of mistrust, a win/lose mentality, tension between faculty and administrators" (Hooker, 1991).

As long as that spirit of mistrust exists, the tension will exist. The mistrust undoubtedly is both symptomatic of and a result of the loss of a sense of community. Among both faculty and administrators, there is clear agreement that community is missing—to the detriment of the entire institution.

In the Möbius strip of reality, community and conflict are intertwined. Where there is a high sense of community, there is low destructive conflict. Where there is little community, there is more conflict. "One of the problems, and the reasons that conflict is so difficult on campuses, is the lack of community. One measure of the extent of community is its capacity to deal creatively with conflict. If they haven't dealt with conflict, they haven't really passed the threshold into community" (Parker Palmer, personal communication, March 14, 1995).

The unique quality of the community is one way in which academic institutions differ from other organizations. "Universities are set apart from other organizations by their members' belief that institutions of higher education are more than schools—they are academic 'communities' " (Folger and Shubert, 1986, p. 5).

More must be done to develop the academic community as a place where all educators—faculty or administrators, student affairs or academic affairs, custodian or vice president, students or trustees—are involved. The academic community needs participation, leadership, and commitment from all sectors. We must give more.

Conclusion

Clark Kerr, an astute observer of the world of higher education, emphasized the importance not only of dealing with the conflicts but of the ways in which we carry out that process. His wisdom from the 1960s rings even more true today: "I see contradictions and conflicts tormenting higher education, as they have so often in the past. I sustain an interest in their effective resolution within the context of this period of history; realizing, in full, that new contradictions and conflicts will arise in the more distant future that we cannot yet even visualize. There are no permanent solutions. How the current contradictions and conflicts work themselves out, and how higher education engages in their resolution, will heavily determine how the future for higher education evolves" (Kerr, 1963, p. xv).

References

Edgerton, R. "Community and Commitment in Higher Education: An Interview with Parker J. Palmer." *AAHE Bulletin*, Sept. 1992, pp. 3–7.

Folger, J. P., and Shubert, J. J. *Resolving Student-Initiated Grievances in Higher Education: Dispute Resolution Procedures in a Non-Adversarial Setting.* National Institute for Dispute Resolution Report No. 3. Washington, D.C.: National Institute for Dispute Resolution, 1986.

Gmelch, W. H., and Carroll, J. B. "The Three Rs of Conflict Management for Department Chairs and Faculty." *Innovative Higher Education*, 1991, 16 (2), 107–123.

Green, M. "Investing in Leadership." *Liberal Education*, 1990, 76 (1), 6–13.

Hooker, M. "Facing Our Challenges." *Change*, May 1991, p. 8.

Kerr, C. *The Uses of the University*. Cambridge, Mass.: Harvard University Press, 1963.

McCarthy, J. "Conclusion." In J. McCarthy (ed.), *Conflict and Mediation in the Academy*. New Directions for Higher Education, no. 32. San Francisco: Jossey-Bass, 1980.

McDade, S. A., and Lewis, P. H. (eds.). *Developing Administrative Excellence: Creating a Culture of Leadership*. New Directions for Higher Education, no. 87. San Francisco: Jossey-Bass, 1994.

SUSAN A HOLTON is professor of communication studies at Bridgewater State College, Bridgewater, Massachusetts, and director of the Massachusetts Faculty Development Consortium.

APPENDIX

CONFLICT MANAGEMENT PROGRAMS IN THE UNITED STATES AND CANADA

Susan A Holton, William C. Warters

Institution and Program Title	Contact Information	Conflict Management Offered	Staff	Eligibility for Services	Funding Level	Program Sponsor
Baltimore City Community College (Baltimore), Student/Faculty Judiciary Committees	McCarroll Nole, Area Director for State and Federal Programs 410-333-7412	Negotiation Judicial processes Formal hearings	Five full-time staff and seven volunteer committee members	All full- and part-time day students	$0	Student Affairs
Boise State University (Boise, Idaho), Training and Development	Gwen Smith, Training and Development Officer 208-385-4418	Mediation				Training and Development
Boise State University (Boise, Idaho), Office of Conflict Management Services	Suzanne McCorkle 208-385-3928	Mediation Negotiation	One part-time secretary		Varies	College of Social Sciences
Briar Cliff College (Sioux City, Iowa), Employee Mediation Program/Grievance Policy and Procedures	Jill Sullivan, Human Resources Officer	Mediation Grievance Policy and procedures	Nine full-time staff: three staff support, three faculty, three administrators	Faculty Staff Administrators	$0–$5,000	President's Office and Board of Trustees
Bridgewater State College (Bridgewater, Mass.), Office of Judicial Affairs	Gerard Stenerson, Assistant to the Vice President, Student Affairs 508-697-1208	Judicial processes	Two full-time staff: assistant to VP student affairs and judicial affairs coordinator residence life	All students Faculty Staff Administrators	$0–$5,000	Student Affairs

Institution and Program Title	Contact Information	Conflict Management Offered	Staff	Eligibility for Services	Funding Level	Program Sponsor
Brigham Young University (Provo, Utah), Off-Campus Housing Mediation and Arbitration Program	H. John Pace 801–378–5066	Mediation Arbitration	Nine full-time staff Seventeen part-time staff One to three volunteers	All students	More than $100,000	Student Affairs
California Institute of Technology (Pasadena, Calif.), Ombuds Office	Helen Hasenfeld, Ombudsperson 818–395–6990	Mediation Negotiation Problem solving	One full-time administrative assistant, one volunteer assistant ombuds person	All students Faculty Administrators Staff Postgraduates	$50,001–$100,000	President's Office
California State University, Fullerton (Fullerton, Calif.), Academic Appeals	Ralph Bigelow, Coordinator 714–773–3836	Mediation Judicial processes	One part-time coordinator	All students	$5,001–$10,000	Student Affairs
California University of Pennsylvania (California, Pa.), CalU-Campus Mediation Center	Alan K. James, Coordinator and Associate Dean of Students 412–936–4439	Mediation Judicial processes	One full-time coordinator, seeking a graduate assistant for assistant coordinator	Anyone in the university community	Currently undetermined	Student Affairs
Canisius College (Buffalo, N.Y.), Campus Mediation Services	Eileen Niland or Nathan Schelble or Patricia Rissmeyer 716–888–2130	Mediation	Three part-time staff and seventeen volunteers	All students Faculty Staff Administrators Community members	$0–$5,000	Office of the Dean of Students

Institution and Program Title	Contact Information	Conflict Management Offered	Staff	Eligibility for Services	Funding Level	Program Sponsor
Carleton University (Ottawa, Ontario, Canada), Mediation Centre	Cheryl Picard, Director 613–788–5765	Mediation Group facilitation Training	One full-time director, one full-time program coordinator, one student worker, thirty volunteer mediators, and three criminology placement students	All students Faculty Staff Administrators Family members Community members	More than $100,000, including salaries	Academic Affairs
Carnegie Mellon University (Pittsburgh), Staff Council Grievance Committee	Human Resources	Under exploration	Volunteer elected committee	Staff at Carnegie Mellon		Office of Human Resources
Case Western Reserve University (Cleveland)	G. Dean Patterson, Jr., Assistant Vice President of Student Affairs 216–368–2020	Counseling University crisis management team	Ten full-time staff	All students Faculty Staff Administrators Family members Community members		Student Affairs, Academic Affairs, Affirmative Action, President's Office, and Administration and Finance
Clark University (Worcester, Mass.)	David Milstone, Dean of Students Office 508–793–7453	Mediation Negotiation Arbitration Judicial processes	Staff already serving	All students Faculty Staff Administrators	$0	Student Affairs

Institution and Program Title	Contact Information	Conflict Management Offered	Staff	Eligibility for Services	Funding Level	Program Sponsor
Clemson University (Clemson, S.C.), Judicial Affairs	Sara Spell, Associate Director of Judicial Affairs 803-656-0510	Mediation Judicial processes	Full-time staff: one associate director, one administrative assistant, two part-time judicial assistants, and two student workers	All students	$0–$5,000, and salaries	Student Affairs
Colorado State University (Fort Collins, Colo.), University Ombudsman Office	William E. King, Ombudsman 303-491-7165		One full-time ombudsman, one full-time administrative assistant, one part-time graduate student	All students Faculty Staff Administrators	$50,001–$100,000	Student Affairs
Columbia University (New York), Ombuds Office	Marsha Wagner 212-854-1234	Mediation Negotiation Shuttle diplomacy	Two full-time staff: ombuds officer and administrative assistant	All students Faculty Staff Administrators Family members Community members	More than $100,000	President's Office
Dartmouth College (Hanover, N.H.), Dartmouth Community Mediation Center	Rabbi Daniel Siegel 603-646-3782	Mediation Negotiation Judicial processes		Full-time day students Graduate students Faculty Administrators Community members	$0–$5,000	Tucker Foundation

Institution and Program Title	Contact Information	Conflict Management Offered	Staff	Eligibility for Services	Funding Level	Program Sponsor
Endicott College (Beverly, Mass.), Grievance Procedures	Susan Koso 508-927-0585, ext. 2029	Mediation Arbitration Negotiation Judicial processes	One part-time director of personnel	Staff	No separate funding	Administration and Finance
Evergreen State College (Olympia, Wash.), Center for Mediation Services	Lynne Stockwell, Program Coordinator 360-866-6000, ext. 6732	Mediation Conciliation Intake services	One part-time coordinator and twenty volunteers	All students	$5,001–$10,000	Student Affairs
Franklin and Marshall College (Lancaster, Pa.), Franklin and Marshall Mediation Center	Gina Butcher, Coordinator (student) 717-291-4390	Mediation Negotiation Judicial processes	Ten volunteers	Full-time day students Faculty Staff	$0–$5,000	Student Affairs
Fresno Pacific College (Fresno, Calif.), Center for Conflict Studies and Peacemaking	Ron Claassen or Dalton Reimer 209-453-2064	Mediation training	Four full-time staff and three part-time staff	Anyone associated with the college	More than $100,000	
George Mason University (Fairfax, Va.), University Dispute Resolution Project	Rachel M. Goldberg, Coordinator 703-993-2887	Mediation Facilitation	One part-time coordinator, eight to ten committee volunteers, and ten to fifteen volunteers	All students Faculty Staff Administrators Family members	$10,001–$25,000	

Institution and Program Title	Contact Information	Conflict Management Offered	Staff	Eligibility for Services	Funding Level	Program Sponsor
Georgia State University (Atlanta), Student Code of Conduct: Judicial System	Kurt Keppler, Dean of Students 404–651–2200 or 651–4082	Judicial processes	Seven full-time staff, two part-time assistant complex directors, and ten judicial board volunteers	All students Faculty Staff Administrators	$0–$5,000	Student Affairs
Georgia State University (Atlanta), Office of the Ombudsperson and Peer Mediation Center	Lin B. Inlow, Ombudsperson 651–2220	Mediation Negotiation Arbitration Judicial processes	One full-time ombudsperson, one part-time secretary, one student employee, one part-time assistant ombuds, nineteen peer mediators-student volunteers	All students Faculty Staff Administrators	$10,001–$25,000/ Ombud $5,001–$10,000/ Peer mediation	Office of the Ombudsperson
Hampshire College (Amherst, Mass.), Conflict, Transformation, and Education Project	Thomas Levitan, Dean of Students 413–582–5412	Mediation Negotiation Facilitation Facilitated discussions	One part-time faculty adviser, two to three coordinator team, and six student volunteers	All students Faculty Staff Administrators	$10,001–$25,000	Student Affairs and President's Office
Hellenic College/Holycross (Brookline, Mass.), Office of Student Life	Archdeacon Gerasimos Michaleas 617–731–3500, ext. 241	Negotiation Judicial processes	Six part-time students and grad students and five student workers	Day students Graduate students	$0–$5,000	Student Affairs
Holyoke Community College (Holyoke, Mass.), College Mediation Team	Isabel Haspaf	Mediation	One part-time staff and twenty volunteers	All students Faculty Staff	$0–$5,000	Student Affairs

Institution and Program Title	Contact Information	Conflict Management Offered	Staff	Eligibility for Services	Funding Level	Program Sponsor
Houston Community College System (Houston), Project ENHANCE	Gilbert C. Ontiveros, Program Manager 713–526–3600	Mediation and conflict management training for staff and faculty				Public Service Contracts
Indiana University (Bloomington), Mediation Services	Naomi Ritter, Academic Associate 812–855–7559	Mediation Negotiation Grievance procedures	One full-time academic associate and four to five part-time associates	All students Faculty Administrators Staff	Undetermined	Affirmative Action
Jefferson Community College (Louisville, Ky.), Ombudsperson	Jill W. Hall, Associate Professor of Communication			All students		Communication Department
John Jay College of Criminal Justice, CUNY (New York), Dispute Resolution Program	Maria R. Volpe, Director 212–237–8693	Mediation Negotiation Dispute resolution	One full-time director and student mediators	All students Faculty Staff	Not applicable	Academic Affairs
Kent State University (Kent, Ohio), Center for Applied Conflict Management	Jennifer Maxwell, Director 216–672–3143		One full-time faculty and two part-time temps	All students Faculty Staff Community members	More than $100,000	Academic Affairs Political Science
Langara College (Vancouver, British Columbia, Canada), Human Rights Coordinator's Office	Brenda E. Taylor, Coordinator 604–323–5640	Mediation Administrative tribunal	One part-time coordinator	All students Faculty Staff Administrators	$50,001–$100,000	President's Office

Institution and Program Title	Contact Information	Conflict Management Offered	Staff	Eligibility for Services	Funding Level	Program Sponsor
Laurentian University (Sudbury, Ontario, Canada), Ombuds Office Labour-Management Committees	Lisetta Chalupiak Personnel Services 717–799–1195					
Lehigh Carbon Community College (Schnecksville, Pa.), Ombudsman		Assist students with faculty complaints	One part-time ombudsman	All students	$10,001–$25,000	Academic Affairs
Macalester College (St. Paul, Minn.), Dispute Resolution/Grievance Procedures	Laurie B. Hamre, Associate Dean of Students 612–696–6220	Mediation Judicial processes	Three part-time college grievance officers, volunteer mediation advisers, and judicial board members	All day students Faculty Staff Administrators Contract staff Union staff	$5,001–$10,000	Student Affairs
Manchester College (North Manchester, Ind.), Manchester College Reconciliation Services	Gary Zimmerman, Chair, Department of Psychology 219–982–5344	Mediation/ conciliation	Two part-time staff: one director and one student Forty volunteer case developers and conciliators	All students Faculty Staff Administrators Family members Community members	$0–$5,000	Student Affairs
Mankato State University (Mankato, Minn.), Mediation Center	Barbara Carson, Department of Sociology 507–389–1561	Mediation Center for info on nonviolent conflict resolution	One full-time staff	All students Faculty Staff Administrators	$50,001–$100,000	Student Affairs and Academic Affairs

Institution and Program Title	Contact Information	Conflict Management Offered	Staff	Eligibility for Services	Funding Level	Program Sponsor
Mankato State University (Mankato, Minn.), Mankato State University Judicial System	Malcolm O'Sullivan, Coordinator of Student Life 507–389–2121	Judicial processes	Two full-time staff, two part-time staff, and one student worker	Anyone associated with the university or community	$50,001–$100,000	Student Affairs
Massachusetts Institute of Technology (Cambridge, Mass.), Mediation@MIT	Laura McDonald and Carol Orme-Johnson, Codirectors 617–253–8720	Mediation		All day students Graduate students Families of students	$10,001–$25,000	Student Affairs
Massachusetts Institute of Technology (Cambridge, Mass.), Ombuds Office, deans' offices, and others	Mary Rowe Ombuds Office	Many different services provided by numerous committees and structures	A dozen people in various capacities	Everyone at the university	More than $100,000	Multiple Auspices
Michigan State University (East Lansing), Office of the Ombudsman	Joy Curtis, Ombudsman 517–353–8830	Mediation Negotiation Judicial processes	Two full-time staff and one part-time staff	All students	More than $100,000	President's Office
Middle Georgia College (Cochran, Ga.), No formal program	Randall Ursrey, Vice President for Student Affairs 912–934–6221					Student Affairs

Institution and Program Title	Contact Information	Conflict Management Offered	Staff	Eligibility for Services	Funding Level	Program Sponsor
North Adams State College (North Adams, Mass.), Campus Community Coordinating Council	Lorraine Maloney 413–662–5285	Mediation	One full-time director of volunteer center and one-quarter time student workers	All students Faculty Administrators Staff Community members	$0–$5,000	Student Affairs
North Central College (Naperville, Ill.), North Central College Dispute Resolution Center	Thomas Cavanaugh, Director 708–637–5157	Mediation Training seminars	One part-time director and two part-time assistant directors	Family members All students Community members	$5,000	Student Affairs and Academic Affairs
North Shore Community College (Danvers, Mass.), Assistant Dean of Students	Thomas Bourne 508–762–4000, ext. 6614	Mediation Judicial processes	Full-time dean and assistant dean of students	All students Faculty Staff Administrators Families of students Community members		Student Affairs
North Shore Community College (Danvers, Mass.), Employee Assistance Program	Judy Gould, Coordinator 508–762–4000, ext. 5546	Mediation Negotiation Arbitration Judicial processes	One part-time coordinator	Faculty Staff Administrators Families of the above Graduate students	$10,001–$25,000	Human Resources
Northern Arizona University (Flagstaff, Ariz.), University Ombuds Office	Earl Backman, Ombudsman 602–523–9358	Mediation Negotiation	One full-time ombudsman and one full-time administrative assistant	Faculty Staff Administrators	More than $100,000	Academic Affairs

Institution and Program Title	Contact Information	Conflict Management Offered	Staff	Eligibility for Services	Funding Level	Program Sponsor
Northern Illinois University (DeKalb, Ill.), Employee Wellness and Assistance Program	Deborah Haliczer, Coordinator 815–753–9191	Mediation	Full-time staff: one coordinator, one assistant coordinator, one part-time graduate program assistant, and one volunteer	Faculty Staff Administrators Family members of the above	$50,001–$100,000	President's Office
Northern Illinois University (DeKalb, Ill.), Office of the Ombudsman	Tim Griffin 815–753–1414	Mediation Negotiation Consultation	One full-time ombudsman, one full-time administrative assistant, and two part-time student ombudspersons	All students Faculty Staff Administrators Family members Community members	$50,001–$100,000	President's Office
Northern Illinois University (DeKalb, Ill.), Provost's Office	Natalie Loder Clark 815–753–1898	Mediation Negotiation Judicial processes	Two full-time staff, one part-time staff	Faculty Staff Administrators	More than $100,000	Academic Affairs
Norwich University (Northfield, Vt.), Honor Council	Martha Mathis 802–485–2640	Mediation Judicial processes	One part-time staff, three student workers, and twenty-five volunteer Honor Council members	All day students Faculty Administrators	$0–$5,000	Student Affairs
Nova Southeastern University (Ft. Lauderdale, Fla.), Conflict Resolution Resource Service	Bill Warters, Director 305–424–5703	Mediation Conciliation and referrals	Two part-time program coordinators	All students Administrators Faculty Staff Community members	$10,001–$25,000	Department of Dispute Resolution

Institution and Program Title	Contact Information	Conflict Management Offered	Staff	Eligibility for Services	Funding Level	Program Sponsor
Ohio University (Athens), University Ombudsman	N. Bain 614–593–2627	Mediation Shuttle diplomacy Intermediation	One part-time ombuds and one part-time assistant ombuds	All day students Graduate students Faculty Staff Administrators	$50,001–$100,000	Independent but reports to Academic Affairs for budget
Oregon State University (Corvallis), Student Conduct and Mediation Program, Office of the Dean of Students	Bill Oye, Coordinator 503–737–3658	Mediation Negotiation Arbitration Judicial processes Conciliation	One full-time coordinator	All students Faculty Staff Administrators Families of students Community members	$10,001–$25,000	Student Affairs
Portland State University (Portland, Oreg.), Campus Ombuds Office	John Wanjala, Ombudsperson 503–725–4472	Informal mediation and negotiation	One full-time ombudsperson and one part-time official specialist staff person	All students Faculty Staff Administrators Community members	$50,001–$100,000	President's Office
Province of Alberta (Edmonton, Alberta, Canada), Ombudsman	Harley Johnson, Ombudsman 404–427–2756	Negotiation Investigation and referrals	Eighteen full-time assistants and three student workers	Community members	More than $100,000	Legislative Assembly
Rice University (Houston), Several programs	Patricia M. Bass, Ombudsperson to students 713–527–4998	Mediation Judicial processes		All students Faculty Staff Administrators		Student Affairs and Affirmative Action

Institution and Program Title	Contact Information	Conflict Management Offered	Staff	Eligibility for Services	Funding Level	Program Sponsor
St. Elizabeth School of Nursing (Utica, N.Y.), Two-year AAS Nursing	Sister Walter Marie, Director 315–798–8125			All students Faculty		Committees
St. Joseph's College (Windham, Maine)	Sister Mary E. Murphy, Dean of the College 207–892–6766	Mediation Negotiation Arbitration Judicial processes Grievance committee		All students Faculty Administrators	$0–$5,000	Student Affairs and President's Office
Saint Mary's College (Notre Dame, Ind.), Student Judicial Board	Suzie Orr, Director of Residence Life and Housing 219–284–4522	Mediation Negotiation Judicial processes	Three part-time board advisers	All day students	$0–$5,000	Student Affairs
St. Olaf College (Northfield, Minn.), Student Conduct System	Matt Hecker, Associate Dean of Services 507–646–3023	Mediation Judicial processes		All full-time day students	$0–$5,000	Student Affairs
St. Olaf College (Northfield, Minn.), Mediation	Shoonie Harwitz 507–646–3368	Mediation	All voluntary	All day students Faculty Staff Administrators		President's Office
Siena College (Loudonville, N.Y.), Human Rights Policy and Procedures	Joyce Legere, Chair 518–783–2532	Mediation Judicial processes	Twenty-four volunteers	All students Faculty Staff Administrators	$0–$5,000	President's Office

Institution and Program Title	Contact Information	Conflict Management Offered	Staff	Eligibility for Services	Funding Level	Program Sponsor
Simon Fraser University (Burnaby, British Columbia, Canada), Ombuds Office	Mark Gervin, Ombudsofficer (student) 604–291–4563	Mediation Negotiation Judicial processes	One full-time ombudsofficer (staff) and one part-time ombudsofficer (student)	All students Faculty Staff Administrators	$50,001–$100,000	Independent
Southern Illinois University (Carbondale), University Ombudsman	Ingrid Clarke, Director 618–453–2411	Mediation Negotiation Judicial processes	Four full-time professional staff and two part-time graduate assistants	All students Faculty Staff Administrators	More than $100,000	President's Office
Southwest Texas State University (San Marcos), Mediation Program	Mediation Advisory Council 512–245–2370	Mediation		All students Faculty Staff Administrators	$5,001–$10,000	President's Office
Stockton College of New Jersey (Stockton), Campus Mediation Program	Linda Rhinier, Associate Director of Housing and Residence Life 609–652–4332	Mediation Judicial processes	One full-time associate director of housing & residence life	All day students	0–$5,000	Student Affairs
State University of New York (Geneseo), Campus Mediation Center	Jim Allen	Mediation	One volunteer Mediation Center administrator	All students Faculty Staff Administrators	0–$5,000	Department of Psychology/free-standing
Syracuse University (Syracuse, N.Y.), Program on the Analysis and Resolution of Conflicts	Robert Rubenstein 315–443–2367	Seminars and training	Two full-time and four part-time staff		More than $100,000	Maxwell School of Citizenship and Public Affairs

Institution and Program Title	Contact Information	Conflict Management Offered	Staff	Eligibility for Services	Funding Level	Program Sponsor
Syracuse University (Syracuse, N.Y.), Campus Mediation Center	Neil H. Katz 315–443–2367	Mediation	Two part-time staff and one student worker	Anyone associated with the university	$10,001–$25,000	Component of the Program on the Analysis and Resolution of Conflicts
Syracuse University (Syracuse, N.Y.), Conflict Resolution Consulting Group	Neil H. Katz 315–443–2367	Training Facilitation Consultation	Two part-time staff and one student worker	All students Faculty Staff Administrators	$10,001–$25,000	Component of the Program on the Analysis and Resolution of Conflicts
Texas A&M University (College Station), Employee Assistance Program	Carolyn A. Raffa 409–845–3711	Mediation for faculty and staff Several others for students	Two full-time staff: director and secretary Two part-time counselors	Graduate students Staff Families of faculty, staff, administrators	More than $100,000	President's Office and Vice-President of Finance and Administration
Texas A&M University (College Station), Student Conflict Resolution Center	Bridget Jackson, Coordinator 409–847–7272	Mediation Negotiation Judicial processes	Seven full-time staff	Anyone involved in a conflict involving a currently enrolled student	More than $100,000	Student Affairs
University at Albany (Albany, N.Y.), University at Albany Dispute Mediation Center	Karleen Karlson Fax: 518–447–5835	Mediation	One full-time director and forty volunteer mediators	All students Faculty Staff Administrators Family members Community members	Undetermined	Student Affairs

Institution and Program Title	Contact Information	Conflict Management Offered	Staff	Eligibility for Services	Funding Level	Program Sponsor
University of Arkansas (Monticello), University Judicial System	Gary Gaston 501–460–1045	Mediation Judicial processes	Two full-time staff: the dean of students and the director of residence life	All students	$0–$5,000	Student Affairs
University of California (Irvine), University Ombudsman Office and Faculty and Staff Assistance Program	Ron Wilson, Assistant Executive Vice Chancellor and Ombudsman 714–824–7256	Mediation Negotiation Arbitration Judicial processes	Five full-time employees and one student worker	Not available	More than $100,000	President's Office
University of California (Los Angeles), Campus Ombuds Office	Howard Gadlin, Ombudsperson 310–825–7627	Mediation Investigation Assessment Facilitation workshops	Four full-time staff, three part-time staff, and one volunteer	All students and families Faculty Staff Administrators	More than $100,000	Student Affairs
University of California (San Diego), Employee Relations	Mary Ann Mead 619–534–4115	Employee relations Public relations and liaison Conflict resolution training	Four full-time staff: manager and three employee relations specialists	Staff Administrators	More than $100,000	Human Resources
University of California (Santa Cruz), Office of the Ombudsman	Sheila K. Gottehrer, Ombudsman 408–459–2073	Mediation Facilitation Shuttle Diplomacy Arbitration Judicial processes	Two full-time staff: ombudsman and assistant ombudsman	All students Faculty Staff Administrators Families of students	Unknown	Chancellor's Office (chancellor's executive assistant)

Institution and Program Title	Contact Information	Conflict Management Offered	Staff	Eligibility for Services	Funding Level	Program Sponsor
University of Cincinnati (Cincinnati), Grievance Procedures	Cynthia Berryman-Fink 513-556-4691	Mediation	Approximately twenty volunteers per year comprised of associate deans and faculty	Faculty	$0–$5,000	Faculty Affairs
University of Colorado (Boulder), Ombuds Office	Tom Sebok, Director 303-492-5077	Mediation Negotiation Workshops and training in a variety of conflict management topics	Three full-time staff: director, associate ombudsperson and administrative assistant, and one student worker	All students Faculty Staff Administrators	More than $100,000	Chancellor's Office (campus CEO)
University of Colorado (Denver), Ombuds Office	Mary Lou Fenili, Assistant Vice Chancellor for Academic and Student Affairs and Ombuds Officer 303-556-4493	Mediation Negotiation	Two part-time co-directors	All day students Graduate students Families of students	$10,001–$25,000	Academic Affairs
University of Delaware (Newark), Judicial Affairs	Nancy Geist Giacomini 302-831-2116	Judicial processes	Three full-time staff and two volunteers	All students	No specific funds for mediation	Student Affairs
University of Houston, Clear Lake (Houston)	Peter Bowman 713-283-3125	Mediation Negotiation Training Environmental facilitation	One full-time director	Full-time and part-time day students Graduate students		School of Business and Public Administration

Institution and Program Title	Contact Information	Conflict Management Offered	Staff	Eligibility for Services	Funding Level	Program Sponsor
University of Houston (Houston), A. A. White Dispute Resolution Institute	E. Wendy Trachte-Huber, Executive Director 713-743-4423	Mediation Negotiation	Three full-time staff, three part-time staff, and twenty-plus volunteers		More than $100,000	Independent non-profit organization
University of Iowa (Iowa City), Faculty and Staff Services	Jim Goldman, Manager 319-335-2085	Mediation Negotiation	One full-time manager and one part-time program assistant	Faculty Staff Administrators Families of the above	More than $100,000	Administration and Finance
University of Iowa (Iowa City), University of Iowa Ombudsperson's Office	Nancy Hauserman, Ombudsperson 319-335-3608	Mediation Negotiation	One full-time associate ombudsperson and one part-time secretary	All students Faculty Staff	More than $100,000	President's Office
University of Manitoba (Winnipeg, Manitoba, Canada), University Mediation Service	Dan Bradshaw 204-474-6634	Mediation	One part-time program coordinator and nine volunteer mediators	All students Faculty Staff Administrators	$0–$5,000	Administration and Finance
University of Manitoba (Winnipeg, Manitoba, Canada), Office of Student Advocacy	Lynn Smith, Director 204-474-7423	Mediation Negotiation Judicial processes	Three full-time staff: director, assistant director, and secretary	All students	More than $100,000	Student Affairs
University of Massachusetts (Amherst), Student Legal Services Office	Charles DiMare 413-545-1995	Mediation Negotiation Judicial processes	Six full-time staff, six attorneys, two support staff, and ten full-time student interns	All students	More than $100,000	Student Affairs and student governance organizations

Institution and Program Title	Contact Information	Conflict Management Offered	Staff	Eligibility for Services	Funding Level	Program Sponsor
University of Massachusetts (Amherst), Ombuds Office	Janet Rifkin, Ombudsperson 413–545–0867	Mediation Negotiation Judicial processes	Two full-time staff: assistant ombudsperson and support staff One part-time graduate student and two student workers	All students and families Faculty Staff Administrators and families	More than $100,000	Chancellor's Office
University of Massachusetts (Boston), Graduate Programs in Dispute Resolution	David Matz, Director Gillian Krajewski, Assistant Director 617–287–7421	Mediation in small claims courts in greater Boston Training off and on campus Facilitation of group meetings as requested	Full-time assistant director, administrative assistant, and one and two-thirds faculty full-time	Anyone who needs help can come and see us. We'll try and help or refer.	More than $100,000	Dean of Graduate Studies
University of Massachusetts (Boston), Ombuds Program	Charles Diggs, Acting Director of Affirmative Action 617–287–5780	Mediation Negotiation	Fifteen volunteers comprised of faculty and staff	All students Faculty Staff Administrators	No funding	Affirmative Action
University of Michigan (Ann Arbor), Judicial Adviser/Judicial Affairs	Mary Louise Antieau, Judicial Adviser 313–936–6308	Mediation Judicial processes	Two full-time staff: judicial adviser and student affairs assistant Two part-time graduate interns and ninety volunteers	All students Faculty Staff Administrators Community members		Student Affairs

Institution and Program Title	Contact Information	Conflict Management Offered	Staff	Eligibility for Services	Funding Level	Program Sponsor
University of Michigan (Ann Arbor), Consultation and Conciliation	Sally M. Johnson, Director of Alternative Dispute Services 313-763-1284	Conciliation Consultation	One full-time director, one part-time consultant, and ten volunteers	Faculty Staff Administrators	$10,000 plus salary	Human Resources and Affirmative Action
University of Minnesota (Minneapolis), Student Dispute Resolution Center	Janet C. Morse, Administrative Director and Ombudswoman 612-626-0891	Mediation Negotiation Ombudsman services	Five part-time staff: administrative director, ombudsman, office specialist, and two students	All students Faculty Staff Administrators Family members Community members	$50,001-$100,000	Student Activities
University of Minnesota (St. Paul), Minnesota Extension Service-Grievance Mediation	Kathleen Mangum 612-624-8710	Mediation	One part-time grievance officer for academic department	Faculty Staff	$0-$5,000	Administration
University of Minnesota (Twin Cities), Conflict and Change Department, University Mediation Program	Tom Fiutne 612-625-3046	Mediation Negotiation Organization Conflict management consulting	One part-time coordinator, two student workers, and twenty-one volunteer mediators	Faculty Administrators	$25,001-$50,000	Academic Affairs
University of Missouri (Rolla)	314-341-4292	Mediation Judicial processes	One full-time staff: assistant to the vice chancellor for student affairs	All students		Student Affairs

Institution and Program Title	Contact Information	Conflict Management Offered	Staff	Eligibility for Services	Funding Level	Program Sponsor
University of Nebraska (Kearney), Ombudsperson Office	Atricia Kenagy, Ombudsperson 308–865–8655	Mediation Consultation Referral Intervention	One full-time, three part-time staff, one student worker	All students Faculty Staff Administrators	$50,001–$100,000 total budget	Chancellor's Office
University of New England (Biddeford, Maine), Judicial Process	Shirley Williams, Assistant Dean of Students 207–283–0170, ext. 2272	Mediation Negotiation Judicial processes	Twelve volunteer Judicial Board members and Committee on Discipline members	All students	$0–$5,000	Student Affairs
University of New Mexico (Albuquerque), Mediation Clinic	Kathy Domenic 505–277–1487	Mediation Facilitation	Three volunteers: director, intake manager, and systems manager	All students Faculty Staff Administrators	$0–$5,000	Communication and Journalism Departments
University of Oregon (Eugene), Mediation Program	Jacqueline L. Gibson, Director 503–346–0617	Mediation Negotiation Facilitation	One full-time director, two student workers, one to four volunteer mediators, and one to six student interns as observers	All students	$50,001–$100,000	Student Affairs and student government
University of Tennessee (Knoxville), Conflict Resolution Program	Steven Martin 615–974–4736	Mediation Consultation	One full-time director, one full-time office manager, and five part-time students	All students Faculty Staff Administrators Families of students	More than $100,000	Chancellor's Office and Administration and Finance

Institution and Program Title	Contact Information	Conflict Management Offered	Staff	Eligibility for Services	Funding Level	Program Sponsor
University of Texas (San Antonio), Problem Solving/Conflict Resolution	Norma S. Guerra, Associate Vice President for Administration and Planning 210-691-4664	Mediation Collaborative problem solving	One full-time administrative assistant and one part-time program coordinator	All students Faculty Staff Administrators	$50,001-$100,000	Planning
University of Victoria (Victoria, British Columbia, Canada), Ombudsperson	Kathleen Beattie, Ombudsperson 604-721-8357	Mediation Negotiation Judicial processes (ad hoc in areas such as academic honesty and academic concessions)	One ombudsperson	All of academic community	$36,655 (CAN)	Funded by Students' Society, University of Victoria, under auspices of Ombuds Advisory Board of faculty, professional staff, and students
University of Washington School of Law (Seattle), Mediation Clinic	Lynne A. Cox 206-543-3434	Mediation	One full-time director/lecturer, two part-time case developers/research assistants, twenty-plus mediators, trainers, coaches, program developers, advisers, and attorneys	Anyone is eligible for services	$110,000	Law School Clinical Law Program
University of Waterloo (Waterloo, Ontario, Canada), University Conflict Resolution Group	Matthew Erickson, Coordinator of Office of Ethical Behaviour and Human Rights 519-888-4567, ext. 3765	Mediation	Fifteen volunteer students, staff, and faculty	Anyone associated with the university is eligible for services including family members and community members	$0-$5,000	Educational Equity

Institution and Program Title	Contact Information	Conflict Management Offered	Staff	Eligibility for Services	Funding Level	Program Sponsor
University of Waterloo (Waterloo, Ontario, Canada), PALS Peer Mediation	Dawn Nyseck 519–885–1211	Mediation Negotiation Conflict support Shuttle diplomacy	Seven to thirteen volunteer peer mediators	All students	$0–$5,000	Federation of Students' Peer Assistant Links Program
University of Western Ontario (London, Ontario, Canada), Office of the Ombudsperson	Frances Bauer 519–661–3573	Informal mediation	One full-time ombudsperson, one full-time assistant ombudsperson	All students	More than $100,000 which includes 2 salaries	University and Student Council contribute equally
University of Western Ontario and Fanshawe College (London, Ontario, Canada), Housing Mediation Service	Glenn Matthews, Housing Mediation Officer 519–661–3787	Mediation Information and counseling	One full-time housing mediation officer and one part-time secretary	All students Landlords related to off-campus housing	$50,001–$100,000	Administration and Finance
University of Windsor (Windsor, Ontario, Canada), Ombudsperson and Race Relations Office	Sushas Ramdioran 519–253–4232	Mediation Negotiation Investigation	One part-time secretary	All students	$25,001–$50,000	Independent Office
Washington State University (Pullman), Office of the University Ombudsman	Mary Gallway, University Ombudsman 509–335–1195	Mediation Negotiation Advice Recommendations Investigation	One full-time assistant to ombudsman; one part-time ombudsman, and one part-time student associate ombudsman	All students Faculty Staff Administrators	$50,001–$100,000	Provost's Office

Institution and Program Title	Contact Information	Conflict Management Offered	Staff	Eligibility for Services	Funding Level	Program Sponsor
Western Connecticut State University (Danbury), Center for Collaboration, Campus Conflict Resolution Project	R. Averell Manes 203–837–8452	Intervention Mediation Negotiation Facilitation and training	One part-time director, volunteers	All students, faculty, staff and families, and people in community	$0–$5,000	Ancell School of Business
Western Illinois University (Macomb), University Ombudsman	309–298–1208	Negotiation Referrals Interpretation of policies	Two part-time staff: clerk and secretary	Anyone associated with the university is eligible for services including community members	$50,001–$100,000	Academic Affairs
Western Michigan University (Kalamazoo), University Ombudsman	Thomas C. Bailey 616–387–5300	Mediation Negotiation Informal alternative dispute resolution	One full-time ombudsman and one full-time administrative assistant	All students and family members Faculty Staff Administrators	More than $100,000, including salaries	President's Office
Western Oregon State College (Monmouth), Campus Judicial Affairs Program	Michael Walsh, Coordinator of Campus Judicial Affairs 503–838–8221	Mediation Arbitration Judicial processes	One volunteer coordinator and six volunteer mediators	All students Faculty Staff Administrators	$0–$5,000	Student Affairs
Wheelock College (Boston), Academic Appeals Board; Hearing Committee; Student Conduct Board	617–734–5200	Mediation Negotiation Judicial processes		All students Faculty Staff Administrators		Student Affairs, Academic Affairs, and Affirmative Action

Institution and Program Title	Contact Information	Conflict Management Offered	Staff	Eligibility for Services	Funding Level	Program Sponsor
Worcester Polytechnic Institute (Worcester, Mass.), Campus Judicial System	Janet Richardson, Assistant Vice President for Student Affairs 508-831-5201	Mediation Judicial processes		All students Faculty Staff Administrators Community members	$0-$5,000	Student Affairs
Wright State University (Dayton, Ohio), Ombuds Office	Kelly Shuman, Ombuds 513-873-5507	Mediation Judicial processes Investigation Facilitation	One part-time ombuds, one part-time assistant, two part-time students	All students Faculty Staff Administrators	$5,001-$10,000	Student Affairs
Wright State University (Dayton, Ohio), Judicial Affairs	Brenda Mitchner, Coordinator of Judicial Affairs 513-873-4172	Mediation Judicial processes	One full-time coordinator and volunteer judicial review board members	All students Faculty Staff Administrators	$25,001-$50,000	President's Office Student Affairs
York University (North York, Ontario, Canada), University Complaint Centre	Debra Glass, Director of Student Affairs 416-736-5144	Mediation Negotiation Judicial processes	Three full-time staff	All students Faculty Administrators Staff		Student Affairs

Note: For a narrative explicating these programs, please contact Susan A Holton, Maxwell Library, Bridgewater State College, Bridgewater, MA 02325; telephone: 508-697-1750, fax: 508-697-1729, e-mail:

INDEX

Weick, K. E., 37, 48
Wentz, D., 38
Whitt, E. J., 44, 45
Williams, D., 11, 12, 13, 14
Williams, M. S., 1
Wilmot, W. W., 27
Wilson, R., 16
Witherspoon, R., 75
Women: campus conflict and, 15; early

admission to universities of, 14–15; obstacles for, 15; sexual harassment of, 15
Workplace relationship conflict: resolution consequences, 30; resolution options, 29–30; vignette, 29

Yale University, 12, 13, 15

ORDERING INFORMATION

NEW DIRECTIONS FOR HIGHER EDUCATION is a series of paperback books that provides timely information and authoritative advice about major issues and administrative problems confronting every institution. Books in the series are published quarterly in Spring, Summer, Fall, and Winter and are available for purchase by subscription and individually.

SUBSCRIPTIONS for 1995 cost $48.00 for individuals (a savings of 37 percent over single-copy prices) and $64.00 for institutions, agencies, and libraries. Please do not send institutional checks for personal subscriptions. Standing orders are accepted. (For subscriptions outside of North America, add $7.00 for shipping via surface mail or $25.00 for air mail. Orders *must be prepaid* in U.S. dollars by check drawn on a U.S. bank or charged to VISA, MasterCard, or American Express.)

SINGLE COPIES cost $19.00 plus shipping (see below) when payment accompanies order. California, New Jersey, New York, and Washington, D.C., residents please include appropriate sales tax. Canadian residents add GST and any local taxes. Billed orders will be charged shipping and handling. No billed shipments to post office boxes. (Orders from outside North America *must be prepaid* in U.S. dollars by check drawn on a U.S. bank or charged to VISA, MasterCard, or American Express.)

SHIPPING (SINGLE COPIES ONLY): $10.00 and under, add $2.50; to $20.00, add $3.50; to $50.00, add $4.50; to $75.00, add $5.50; to $100.00, add $6.50; to $150.00, add $7.50; over $150.00, add $8.50.

DISCOUNTS FOR QUANTITY ORDERS are available. Please write to the address below for information.

ALL ORDERS must include either the name of an individual or an official purchase order number. Please submit your order as follows:
    Subscriptions: specify series and year subscription is to begin
    Single copies: include individual title code (such as HE82)

MAIL ALL ORDERS TO:
    Jossey-Bass Publishers
    350 Sansome Street
    San Francisco, California 94104-1342

FOR SUBSCRIPTION SALES OUTSIDE OF THE UNITED STATES, contact any international subscription agency or Jossey-Bass directly.

OTHER TITLES AVAILABLE IN THE
NEW DIRECTIONS FOR HIGHER EDUCATION SERIES
Martin Kramer, Editor-in-Chief